MW00966094

YOU'RE GOING TO BE OK:

Real Hope for Fighters of Cancer, Mental Illness, Sexual Abuse, or Loss

BOB JONES

DEDICATION

Dedicated to supporting the brave fighters of cancer, mental illness, sexual abuse, loss, and trauma. You are not alone.

Dedicated to Sharon Atkins, Bob's cousin, who lost her battle with mental illness. You are not forgotten.

"You're going to be OK." – may be the exact words you need to hear. By reading these beautiful stories that Bob Jones has masterfully collected from women who have walked these difficult and dark roads, you will hear each unique voice encouraging you with hope, comfort, and courage. Remember, sweet one, God will restore the years the locust has eaten.

  - Cyana Gaffney, Author and speaker.

During my darkest days how I wish I had a voice in my ear shouting "You're Going To Be OK!". This is that voice. Testimonies have power, and Author Bob Jones has created a remarkable compilation of amazing women who have overcome some of the most hopeless situations. This book will be a piercing light of hope in the hands of someone desperate to know if they're going to be ok.

  - Sarah E. Ball, Author of Fearless in 21 Days, Cochrane, Alberta

Life is a unique blending of pain and sorrow, of joy and laughter. This book contains this unique blend in the stories of eleven courageous women who faced their pain and suffering with tenacity and hope. Brutally honest, they share their fears and intense struggles with their hard life realities. Yet, there is no hint of self-pity or making their pain a shrine. These wickedly strong women are hope-lifters and will encourage their readers to embrace and live in the transforming power of hope.

  - Margaret Gibb – Women Together

CONTENTS

FOREWORD – SUSAN WELLS

You are not in this alone. The honesty of the women within these pages made me feel like I had made new friends. Their raw accounts of facing crippling physical and emotional issues are beautifully woven so that anyone can relate.

"You're Going to be OK" doesn't throw out shallow platitudes or easy formulas. Rather, you are lovingly guided along the path that eleven women have travelled to reach their wholeness. You have permission to feel sad, be mad, get angry, but you will not be left on your own. Their course of actions had set them free and now they are offering hope for others. If they could do it, so can you.

Don't let the subject matter hold you back. You'll feel compassion and saddened at times, but I promise you will leave strengthened and encouraged! You might grab a tissue to wipe away a tear, but you may soon find yourself sopping up the waterworks from uproarious laughter.

With each account, the faces of friends popped into my mind. "You must read this", resonated over and over. Your story may not look exactly like the ones here, but the life principles shared, and encouragement offered are like the writer says in Proverbs 25:11, "A word spoken at the right time is like gold apples in silver settings".

Bob Jones, the "dispenser of hope" has masterfully relayed the stories of others, but, there's much more here. During our thirty years of friendship I've watched him overcome insurmountable challenges. I'd ask my husband, David, in the midst of the battle, "Can it possibly get any worse?" At the same time, we watched Bob selflessly walk alongside others facing deep crises. Bob has not only personally overcome; he has used his life experience to continue his mission of reassurance. His heart for the hurting resonates on every page.

This is truthful story telling at its best. A treasure awaits you.

BOB JONES

INTRODUCTION

Bob and Jocelyn Jones – REVwords

Hope is the thing with feathers that perches in the soul and sings the tune without words and never stops at all.
~ Emily Dickinson

January snow was falling back home in St Albert, Alberta, noses were freezing, and people were dreaming about sand, sun, and surf. Jocelyn was living the dream.

Not that long ago her choice of a winter holiday anywhere in the world was a Rockie mountain high. Skiing - or sunning – on the slopes of Lake Louise, Sunshine Village or Marmot Basin were her happy places.

Now the smell of the ocean, the warmth of the Caribbean sun, a good book and a reclining chair on the 14th deck of the Royal Caribbean's Navigator of the Seas replaced the slopes, skis, and poles. What could be more serene?

"You're going to be OK."

The sound was so solid she turned in her recliner to see who was speaking. Left, then right. She was alone. The words sounded like a fading echo, "You're going to be OK."

She was already OK. More than OK. Is the ship going to sink? Why would I need to be OK?

Bob is going to die. That can't be - he's too young and healthy. What if he did die? "You're going to be OK."

What did this mean? There was no fear. Just weirdness. And calm.

Was this God speaking? If so, being OK is a good thing.

All right then, everything was going to be OK.

Two months later, the unexpected happened. The voice at the other end of the phone uttered three words that changed everything. "This can't be happening to me. Where's Bob?" And then the sound started pulsating. It wasn't her heartbeat. The words from the sunshine of the 14th deck echoed into her mind.

"You're going to be OK."

Have you received a similar phone call? The worst news you could ever imagine. Your very life is under siege.

You're overwhelmed.

You feel scared.

You're fighting for air.

If your world is a mess, it doesn't mean that you have to be one.

You were in our thoughts and our prayers when we wrote this book.

Words matter.

A book can be an answer to a prayer.

There is one thing we offer you.

Without this one thing, even the smallest tasks, let alone life and death issues are impossible.

Without this one thing couples give up on their marriage, parents give up on their teens, leaders give up on their people, and people give up on their future.

You can survive for 40 days without food, about 3 days without water, and about 8 minutes without air.

You don't want to go a single second without this one thing. That one thing is HOPE.

That's why Jocelyn and I envision ourselves as hope dispensers. We've experienced the power of hope in our lives and are sharing it freely with others.

You are hardwired for hope.

Every decision you make, every response you have to situations and relationships in your life is motivated by hope.

Your story is a hope story.

Your happiest moments are hope moments.

Your saddest moments are about hope dashed.

You're always looking for hope.

You're always attaching the hope of your heart to something.

With hope anything is possible. Without hope, you lose your ability to breathe.

Sometimes you need to hang on to someone else's hope. Someone else's peace and sanity while yours is under siege.

Do it.

Courage, hope, faith, sanity, peace - they all come and go. Borrow them from someone else's supply until your own comes back in.

We share real stories of eleven women – our friends - who fight cancer, sexual abuse, mental illness, and loss. They borrowed what we share with you – a way forward - a way to find meaning and hope through the suffering.

Each woman opened a window on a moment of her experience.

Their stories are raw and honest, and you won't find a pretty bow at the end of some chapters. But you will find hope. They use faith, medication, prayer, physicians, forgiveness, and therapy as God's gifts for healing.

Real hope is not wishful thinking. Hope is not whistling in the dark or plugging your ears to shut out reality.

Hope is not pretending problems don't exist.
Hope is the belief problems won't last forever.

Hurts will be healed.

Difficulties will be overcome.

Hope is an anchor of the soul, sure and steadfast. Anchors serve best in stormy weather.

Hope is holding on to what gives life meaning and being safely anchored by that meaning against life's storms.

Near the village of Gonia on a rocky bay of the island of Crete, sits a Greek Orthodox monastery. Alongside it, on land donated by the monastery, is an institute dedicated to human understanding and peace, and especially to rapprochement between Germans and Cretans. An improbable task, given the bitter residue of wartime.

This site is important because it overlooks the small airstrip at Maleme where Nazi paratroopers invaded Crete and peasants attacked them wielding kitchen knives and hay scythes. The retribution was terrible. The populations of whole villages were lined up and shot for assaulting Hitler's elite troops.

High above the institute is a cemetery with a single cross marking the mass grave of Cretan partisans. And across the bay on yet another hill is the regimented burial ground of the Nazi paratroopers. The memorials were placed that all might see and never forget. Hate was the only weapon the Cretans had at the end, and it was a weapon many vowed never to give up.

Against this heavy curtain of history, in this place where the stone of hatred is hard and thick, the existence of an institute devoted to healing the wounds of war is a fragile paradox. How has it come to be here? The answer is a man. Dr. Alexander Papaderos.

He was a doctor of philosophy, teacher, politician, and resident of Athens. At war's end, he came to believe that the Germans and the Cretans had much to give one another. They had an example to set. For if they could forgive each other and construct a productive relationship, then any people could.

Dr. Papaderos liked to explain the meaning of life by telling one of his wartime stories.

Taking his wallet out of his hip pocket, he would fish into a leather billfold and bring out a tiny, round mirror, about the size of a quarter. And what he said went like this:

"When I was a small child, during the war, we were destitute, and we lived in a remote village. One day, on the road, I found the broken pieces of a mirror from a German motorcycle wreckage.

I tried to find all the pieces and put them together, but it was not possible, so I kept only the largest one. And by scratching it on a stone, I made it round. I began to play with it as a toy and became fascinated by the fact that I could reflect light into dark places where the sun would never shine - in deep holes and crevices and dark closets. It became a game for me to get light into the most inaccessible places I could find.

I kept the little mirror, and as I went about my growing up, I would take it out in idle moments and continue the challenge of the game. As I became a man, I grew to understand that this was not just a child's game but a metaphor for what I might do with my life. I came to realize that I am not the light or the source of the light. But light - truth, understanding, knowledge - is there, and it will only shine in dark places if I reflect it.

I am a fragment of a mirror whose whole design and shape I do not know. Nevertheless, with what I have, I can reflect light into the dark places of this world - into the black places in the hearts of men - and change some things in some people. Perhaps others may see and do likewise. That is what I am about. This is the meaning of my life."

We become powerful when we share our stories of hope.

Let the eleven stories in this book reflect the light of forgiveness, hope, and love into the dark places of your experience.

Lin Yutang, a renowned Chinese thinker, wrote in 1959, "Hope is like a road in the country; there was never a road, but when many people walk on it, the road comes into existence."

You have a compass, and the following stories provide the road. Once you've walked the road, you'll want to share it with those you love.

"You're going to be OK."

Hope is the reason for the New Testament section of the Bible. Some of the last words in a letter written to Christian believers under siege in Rome were a prayer.

We've co-opted the prayer as our heart for you.

"I pray that God, the source of hope, will fill you completely with joy and peace because you trust in him. Then you will overflow with confident hope..." Romans 15:13 (New Living Translation)

You're going to be OK.

CHAPTER ONE

Glori Meldrum – Be Brave

It is important for me to share my experiences in order to create strength and hope for others. No matter how far down you go, it is never too late to come back.
~ Theo Fleury

Hope is not blind optimism. It's not ignoring the enormity of the task ahead, or the roadblocks that stand in our path. It's not sitting on the sidelines or shirking from a fight. Hope is that thing inside us that insists, despite all the evidence to the contrary, that something better awaits us if we have the courage to reach for it, work for it, and fight for it.
~ Barack Obama

By age 12, I was having thoughts of suicide. There's nothing easy about being a survivor of child sexual abuse. You have lots of shame and not a lot of self-love. The biggest thing that survivors want to know is that there's hope to get better and to understand how they can get there. Even though you may have had a traumatic life, which I did, you can still be happy.

In 2007, I founded *Little Warriors*, an Edmonton-based, national non-profit agency that works to prevent child sexual abuse. I was one of those kids. I'm a little warrior myself.

We have four children, including an adopted son from Ethiopia. My husband Gary and I traveled to Ethiopia four times to do volunteer work. For me, it's about making a difference. I love being of service, and I love helping people.

Like most people, my childhood shaped the person I was to become later in life. My parents split up when I was two-years-old, and there was a severe disparity in their incomes.

My father was a businessman who had a knack for making money and began buying apartment buildings in our hometown of Miramichi, New Brunswick. When we spent time together, we would always eat supper at a restaurant.

My mother had a heart of gold and worked hard for every cent she earned. But, even with two jobs, pumping gas and working in a grocery store, mom couldn't afford the luxury of taking us out to a restaurant.

Over the years, my father helped me appreciate the world of business and become familiar with earning money. I suppose he was my first employer; when I was a child, he would pay me ten dollars to read a book. Early in life, I decided to emulate the traits I admired in my father. I wanted to have his business smarts so I could provide for my family and afford some of the luxuries in life without having to worry.

Had I been smarter, I would have also chosen to borrow a trait from my mother – her kindness. Adopting something that precious would have served me well, but I was destined to learn that particular lesson the hard way, and later in life.

Another person who influenced my formative years was my grandfather, a serial pedophile who sexually abused me for over two years, starting when I was only eight years old.

From the examples of my father, I learned ambition, resolve, and what it means never to give up. He also liked to ask me questions and challenge me in our dinnertime debates, which taught me how to think analytically.

From the trauma of my grandfather, I was left feeling fearful, angry, and bitter. He had stolen everything from me and created a pattern of anxiety that would haunt me for decades. I promised myself a man would never again control me.

The aftermath of my grandfather's crimes was almost as devastating as being molested. My mother believed me when I finally worked up the courage to share my story, but my aunts and uncles did what people do – they blamed the victim. They wondered how I had behaved towards my grandfather and even asked me what I was wearing. Their reaction shocked me and left me feeling hollow and unloved. I began counting the days until I could leave Miramichi.

The next major turning point in my life happened at Dalhousie University. Academic life did not come easily to me – I had to study my ass off to keep up and, because of my motivation, that's what I did. The source of my motivation was my family, but not in the way you might think. It's highly motivating when your extended family tells you all your life that you'll be 'nothing'… and deep down inside, you're determined to be 'something.'

The exciting milestones I spoke of occurred when I signed up for a Marketing class. Not only did I fall in love with marketing, but I also met and fell in love with the sexy beast who would become my husband, Gary Meldrum.

How could I resist? Gary was the only nice guy I had ever dated: charming, funny, smart, and at the heart of his being, a beautiful human being. I thank the big guy above every day for bringing this man into my life.

Flash forward to life after university. Gary and I headed to Edmonton with ten boxes of clothes, a Visa with a $500 limit and $60,000 worth of student loans.
Fortunately, I was able to secure a job with a recruitment firm almost immediately.

That lasted a year.

Then I moved to the exciting world of radio to work in promotions. Because radio offers a fun and dynamic environment, people make sacrifices to work there. I was working 80 hours a week and bringing home $27,500 before taxes.

That lasted a year and a half.

I was just too eccentric to work for anyone else. The only option was to start my own company. This epiphany came to me during one of those 80-hour weeks near the end of my radio career, and without giving myself time to change my mind, I came home and announced the plan to Gary. No surprise – his response was, "Awesome!"

I started g[squared]™ out of our small home in Millwoods and knocked on doors to get people to hire me. I still remember my first clients: K-days, Walls Alive, Safe Kids, and Carmella's Perfumeria. Those were tough days – I hustled, I worked hard, and I hustled some more.

My hard work began to pay off. Within three years of starting g[squared]™, I had achieved the business goals I had set as a young girl. I was on a path of my creation and well on my way to 'having it all.' I had married the man of my dreams, started my own business, and was having phenomenal success. Our revenue at g[squared]™ had grown by 1,300% in the first 12 years.

I had everything I wanted. And still, I was broken. I was sick, all of the time. Sleep usually eluded me, and when I did manage to fall asleep, I would often wake up in a full-blown panic attack. Even when the company was doing well, for some reason, I always needed more. Why? Because I was afraid of losing it, fearful that someone would take it away from me. Fear continued to drive me, and I tried to escape by burying myself further and further into my work. My involvement in everything at work had mixed results. To the outside world, we looked successful; we continued to attract clients, and the clients were pleased with the work we were providing.

The view from inside the company was a different story. As much as it pained me to admit it, g[squared]™ had become a revolving door because of me. I had no sense of self-love, and because I couldn't love myself, I had no idea how to love or treat others. I drove myself hard, and I was there to drive the rest of the staff until every project was perfect.

Well, I drove them all right. I drove them crazy, and I right out the door. You think I'd be able to see what was happening, but I was having trouble even seeing who I was as a human being. All I did was work and behave like an ass towards people. On top of that, I was 40 pounds too heavy and downright miserable.

With everything I had accomplished, and in spite of all the noise in my head, I could still hear the echoes of my relatives telling me that I was 'nothing'.

The truth is – I was worse than nothing. I was a broken mess.

If I had continued on the same course, it's hard to say where my life would have gone from there. By now, children had come into our lives. I was still managing to hold my precious family together, thanks in large part to the patience and understanding of my wonderful husband. But something had to change. I had to change, and through the most random encounter, an opportunity presented itself.

I had slipped into a Starbucks for a coffee and bumped into an old friend who was also a sexual abuse survivor. She looked great, but at the same time, she was different in a way that I couldn't explain. And then it hit me.

She looked happy.

It was such a foreign concept to me by now that I didn't compliment her or react as most people would. I just stared and said, "Why? Why are you so happy?" Her answer was what I needed to hear.

She and I had come from similar backgrounds of abuse, but it appeared she had found some magic bullet of happiness. When I asked, she shared it with me – she had been through The Hoffman Process. It was a program that took you to the middle of nowhere for seven days with no cell phones and no communication with the outside world. It had given her a new start.

Impulsively, which will come as no shock to anyone who knows me, I signed up. A few weeks later, I was boarding a plane to Hamilton, Ontario. I had no idea what I was getting myself into, but I knew my life needed a drastic change. Although The Hoffman Process is also conducted in a beautiful setting here in

Alberta, I decided to go east because I didn't want to bump into anyone I knew. As broken as I was, my ego still had a lot of pride.

At the airport, I kissed my kids' goodbye, then locked eyes with my husband, Gary. "I promise you," I said, "that I won't come back as the same person." Hours later, I was on the other side of the country checking into The Hoffman Centre and wondering how anyone could undo a lifetime of fear and negativity in 7 days. It didn't take me long to find out.

The Hoffman Process is unlike anything else I have experienced. You work on your emotional wellbeing for sixteen hours a day. Literally, from the time you wake up until the time you pass out, exhausted, you are 'in' the process. Out of respect to The Hoffman Centre and the work they do, I am not going to share much about the profound methods they have developed, but I would like to tell you about the two turning points that aided my evolution.

For me, the first breakthrough happened on day three. We were given plastic bats and told to take our anger out on pillows. It wasn't just a matter of minutes; it went on for hours. We were batting, and yelling, and screaming, and frankly, it felt ridiculous. That kind of violence was not how I expressed myself, and I didn't get the point. So, being a smart girl, I positioned myself beside the loudest, angriest guy in the room and just did whatever he was doing. Yeah, I was smart, but they were smarter. They caught me, and they called me out.

"Why aren't you mad," they asked me. "What happened? What happened to you? What are you not letting go? What are you not dealing with?"

They pushed, and they pushed and, as you've no doubt guessed, they pushed some more. I went to a place I didn't want to go. They pushed me to the deepest recesses of my darkest memories. For years I had managed not to dig that deep into my devastating cave of horrors.

I never wanted to reach that level of pain and be forced to deal with it.

But when it's the only thing you can think about, as your will and your spirit and your body begin to tire, you get there. I got there. And I lost myself in my anger.

My own emotions consumed me. Something inside of me exploded, and I began to rage. This time, I wasn't imitating anyone; I raged and felt the fury build until drenched in sweat. I screamed until I broke, and at the moment of breaking, I had no choice but to embrace the truth – I hated myself.

I did not have an ounce of self-love, and if I didn't love myself, how could I expect anyone else to love me? How could I love anyone else? It was the most humbling moment of my life. I hit bottom.

I had tried so hard to hang on to everything I thought I knew about myself. Even though I hadn't loved that version of me, it was all I knew. But, I wasn't able to. They had broken me. Now, the question was – in the four days we had left, could I possibly heal?

Understand that while the process has its devastating moments, The Hoffman Centre is a great home of kindness, wisdom, and strength. There is a spiritual element that lives through the program and the staff. Never for a moment did I feel unsafe, and I thank them for that. It aided tremendously in the healing.

My second profound experience happened a few days later. We were instructed to 'bury ourselves.' I was sent into the woods alone, in the dead of winter, to find a clearing, lie down and cover myself with a sheet of plastic. Lying there in the bitter cold, it was easy to imagine me as a corpse. The next step in the assignment was determining how I would have died if I had never sought help. As difficult as this is to write, if I'm frank, I felt I would have killed myself by the time I was 44.

Now the hard part. Lying there on the frozen ground, having already admitted an unimaginable ugliness about my existence, I was to envision the people who would attend my funeral and imagine what they would say.

My husband, Gary, floated into view. "Glori, how could you do this to our family?" My body experienced a spasm of pain.

The next faces to appear were from Little Warriors, survivors, support staff, people I love and respect. Warriors – all of them. They appeared as floating, mournful, and behind them, I imagined the hundreds of children in our care. Their message was simple and shattering. "If you can't be healthy, how can we?"

Then, of course, my children. Bless them, they were just babies, and in my vision, they were crying with arms outstretched. "Mommy, we love you. Come back."

I sat up, unable to take any more. Knowing how I would hurt the people I love gave me a new resolve. There was no choice – I had to get better. I had to learn to love myself.

In the following days, with the guidance of The Hoffman Centre staff, I learned to surrender and to let go of the old Glori. I learned to be present in my own life, and I discovered how to look at the world as a child and how to experience joy. In my spiritual travels, I rediscovered the eight-year-old girl I had lost so many years before. She was beautiful, and I loved her.

When I completed the formal portion of The Hoffman Process, I spent two days in a hotel room mentally unpacking everything that had transpired in those long, emotionally exhausting days. It was a 'settling in' time, allowing your soul to absorb what had happened, and giving your mind time to adjust to a new course.

When I arrived home, my kids ran to meet me at the airport, and my oldest said, "Mommy, you look different."

She was right. I was.

But the process was far from over. I had been emotionally scrubbed raw – every sound, every word, every nuance in my life heightened. I had gone from being a zombie to being hyper-aware. As I was trying to adjust and be present in the new path I was on, I suddenly had to face another unexpected crisis. Four of my senior managers, including my best friend, left g[squared]™ to form their own company. It was a devastating blow, professionally and personally. To me, they had been family.

There is no easy way to talk about a breakup; it's always complicated, and there are a million reasons why people do the things they do, but I had to own my part. I had always tried to treat my managers kindly, but they had seen me treat other people poorly and witnessed me carve a path of self-destruction.

In hindsight, this break may have aided my evolution. I was already rebuilding my emotional and personal life; I might as well add my professional life and have a fresh start.

Most of all, it was a chance to put 'leading from love' into practice. I began to see everything from a new place and focused a ton of positive energy into rebuilding my team. Naturally, I wanted to find the most talented people available, but there was more to it than that. I had a vision of where I wanted to be with my life, and I was determined to surround myself with like-minded people. In the interviews, I would ask questions like,

"What was the toughest thing you've been through in your life, and what did it teach you?"

I even changed my approach to finding clients – I wanted to work with people who were positive, upbeat, collaborative, and, above all, respectful. I had lived in a dark pit for so many years I was determined to avoid people who could pull me back in.

As my staff and client base grew, my family life also became richer. Rather than throwing myself into my work, I established a healthy work-life balance and encouraged the same with my co-workers. Learning to love myself meant having more love for everyone around me, and it changed the perspective from which I led my team.

Today, I share the information. If the company is facing a challenge, I let the team know what it is and how we are dealing with it. It's honest and heartfelt and allows the team to be a part of the solution. When we have success stories, and there are many, they belong to the group – all of us.

I empower my team to make their own decisions, and if mistakes happen, we deal with the mistakes. They know I have their backs, and I know they have mine. Our office is full of laughter, and people stay.

Above all, when you lead from a position of love, there is respect and engagement. No more 'going through the motions'… now I establish real connections. I get to know each member of the staff – we celebrate birthdays, anniversaries, births, and other special occasions together.

Since my days as an eight-year-old, faith in God sustained me. Even through the two years, my grandfather abused me, God and church were a part of my life. On Sundays, I sat in the pew beside my grandfather. When the pastor would invite people to come for prayer and ask Jesus into their heart, I was always there. "Dear God, please make him stop."

I know Little Warriors is an answer to the prayers of girls and boys. God is the reason Little Warriors and Be Brave Ranch exist and achieved such incredible success. There's a more significant force behind all the pieces coming together. It's God's love and wisdom that promoted our work on the international stage.

In 2017 a diagnosis of cancer almost broke me. Was this the last straw? The fear, sleepless nights, hospital visits, treatments, follow-up appointments took their toll on our family and me, but we're moving forward. Through it all, I've never stopped believing.

I am anticipating a future from a place of love and optimism, not the place of fear or dread that I was living in on that cold, bleak day in the woods. The journey to love myself continues, and I know I will work on it every day for the rest of my life. It's a lot of hard work, but that precocious eight-year-old girl and the woman she has become are worth it.

Sexual abuse is a burden none should bear, let alone society's most vulnerable and innocent. Child sexual abuse is both heartbreaking and life-changing for the young victims and their families. Sadly, in North America, it has touched millions of lives, often leading to negative lifelong consequences. While the actions can never be taken back, new research from the Faculty of Medicine & Dentistry's Department of Psychiatry is now showing a better path to recovery for the young survivors.

A clinical trial performed at the Little Warriors Be Brave Ranch has confirmed that a four-week intervention program significantly reduces the psychological impacts of child sexual abuse. Our facility is the first of its kind to offer intensive, dedicated, and multi-modal treatment to child sexual abuse survivors aged 8 to 12. The clinical trial evaluated the new treatment model, which provides child survivors with the unique opportunity to access individual and group therapies in a residential environment, alongside peers who have experienced similar trauma.

Results published in the *Journal of Child and Adolescent Behaviour* confirm the program's success, measuring a highly significant reduction in symptoms. This includes a 25 percent reduction in child post-traumatic stress disorder (PTSD) scores, a reduction in the number of children experiencing PTSD (14 children, down from 26) and a significant decrease in depression and anxiety. Forecasts also suggest reduced mental health-related issues and improved outcomes for these children in the future, potentially improving societal and economic outcomes.

"People who have experienced child sexual abuse have much higher rates of problems that affect both their psychological and physical health for many years," explains Peter Silverstone, professor of psychiatry and lead author of the paper. "If you look at the people who subsequently end up on the street or homeless, large numbers of them suffered abuse—physical, sexual, and emotional—as children."

"For the past 20 to 30 years, the primary method has been intermittent treatment. A therapist will meet a survivor every week or two—and the fact of the matter is that it is not the most effective. This study represents a paradigm shift in the way that we suggest children survivors should be treated. This comprehensive approach is making a difference. We are changing the trajectory of children's lives."

The programming at Be Brave Ranch was commissioned by Little Warriors before its construction and developed under Silverstone and Jacqui Linder, an expert traumatologist at City University of Seattle. The purpose-built facility—funded through personal and corporate donations—opened in the fall of 2014 at a location east of Edmonton, welcomes child survivors to its 120-acre setting. Over a year, children participate in 200 hours of therapy along with other therapeutic activities, including structured play, physical exercise, animal interactions, arts and crafts, and music. All operating costs are funded entirely by donations.

There have been so many miracles. Honestly, it has been because of the miracles that we are what we are.

I see the impact the Be Brave Ranch has on the children. The biggest thing you notice about a kid that first comes to the ranch is the void look in their eyes. But after five days, I can see life and light coming back into them. People always ask me what the kids say, and for the most part, the kids can't believe how many people came together to make the program—the whole experience—happen for them. They never knew so many people loved them.

The program that we have at the Be Brave Ranch is the first of its kind. Initially, we faced a lot of criticism about the intensive environment, the kids having to stay there, and if it was all needed. Our clinical trial results confirm everything we have worked for, and we are excited to continue helping children grow into happy, healthy adults.

Dr. Silverstone replicated the model of the Be Brave Ranch for groups of older children, particularly 12- to 16-year-olds. The test results in the areas of PTSD, depression, anxiety, and self-esteem showed marked improvement, similar to what was seen in the younger age groups.

"Short, intense, multi-focal programs work," says Silverstone. "The impact we've seen in just four weeks proves it. And if you look at the relative cost of a four-week program compared to the cost of long-term treatment, I hope that governments recognize you can make a profound difference in a child's life through this intervention."

I know we can do more. We're under-utilizing the Ranch. We can take 60 kids per month easily, and right now we have 10. There's still 100 acres of the Be Brave Ranch that we haven't used yet. So we have a lot of capacity, and we want to use it.

We want to be a centre for excellence and innovation. So when we're seeing a significant demand to help kids between 12 and 16 years old, we want to modify our program so we can treat those kids too and give them the same outcome. Our goal is to heal as many kids from child sexual abuse as possible.

The cost of the program is about $25,000 per youth – ages eight to twelve, and for ages thirteen to sixteen it is $10,000 per youth due to a shorter program. Little Warriors hopes to continue the program free of charge.

- - - - -

Glori Meldrum invited me to be a part of her first *Little Warriors* promotional campaign. I was to wear my Sunday best suit with a red blindfold around my eyes. The caption below the picture read, "Is this how you see child sexual abuse in your community?" I had to admit I was ignorant of the extent and impact of child sexual abuse.

Without Little Warriors, the blindfold may have become a permanent accessory.

Five Facts About The Be Brave Ranch
* *The Be Brave Ranch is a 160-acre property east of Edmonton in Strathcona County.*
* *One in three girls and one in six boys will be sexually abused.*
* *95% of sexual abusers are known and trusted by their victim.*

* *95% of child sexual abuse survivors don't tell anyone about their abuse until they are adults.*
* *70% of sexual abuse survivors report abusing drugs and alcohol.*

In addition to being a Little Warrior herself, Glori is a business owner, mother, wife, and philanthropist. She owns and operates a successful advertising agency. Glori is also involved in several projects for local not-for-profit organizations, including WIN House, Stollery Children's Hospital Foundation, and The Canadian Breast Cancer Foundation.

Glori's hard work hasn't gone unnoticed. She was among the top 18 finalists from 6400 nominees for the 2017 RBC Entrepreneur of the Year Award for Social Change for her work with Little Warriors. She was the recipient of 2011 Canadian Living Me to We Award – Social Action category; Ernst & Young's Entrepreneur of the Year award in the Social Entrepreneur category; the 2009 Rotary Integrity Award; a 2008 Global Woman of Vision award; a 2005 YWCA Woman of Distinction award; was named one of Caldwell Partners' 2010 "Top 40 Canadians Under 40"; and she became the first female president of the Entrepreneur's Organization (EO) of Edmonton.

CHAPTER TWO

Sarah Ball – Fearless

Fear can hold you prisoner. Hope can set you free.
~ Stephen King (*The Shawshank Redemption*)

I ran into the house clammy and panicked.

I didn't want to be alone.

But, I also unquestionably did not want to share my tormenting thoughts with anyone else.

Concerned by my frantic behaviour, my husband asked, "Are you okay?"

"I'm fine," I lied, as I handed off the kids for bedtime.

I hurried to my bedroom.

Panicked, desperate thoughts flooded my conscious. "How does God deal with suicide? Would I go to hell? How would my family deal with it? Would I ever actually have the guts to do it?"

I locked my door, longing to leave these forceful thoughts on the other side of it, but they followed me to my bed, the place I always ran to when I was afraid, the place I had been spending most of my days. I grabbed my Bible and flung it open, desperate for God to jump out and hold me and promise me everything was going to be okay.

How did I get here?

Sixteen years earlier, my life was a disaster. I was a single mom of two small children, living in poverty, abandoned, and afraid. However, this was the moment in my life that I began trusting God for my basic needs, and He began turning my life around. Soon God opened wide a door for me to go to University. Five years later, I graduated with honors, met and married my wonderful husband, bought my first home, became a ministry leader and a writer, and had three more children! I began to see that God's promises were true. His goodness blew me away, and my passion for Him exploded!

One day at a church conference, a woman I highly respected, prayed over me and told me that she felt God was going to entrust me with a deliverance ministry in the area of mental illness, anxiety, depression, and OCD. It was an interesting word, not a direction I ever thought of myself going in. I was a mommy blogger and rarely struggled with depression, or so I thought.

A few years after that prayer, I got tired, really tired.

Tiredness turned into burnout, and that burnout turned into depression, and then one day, after a season of trials I couldn't get out of bed, I couldn't drive my kids to school, or cook dinner, or shower, because I was mentally ill.

I began having panic attacks that turned into a full-blown panic disorder. Anxiety was never something I struggled with in the past. I was a mom of five, a ministry leader, a mentor and a self-proclaimed "suck it up princess," "gett'r done," "hustle hard girl." Then I developed a life-changing anxiety disorder, panic disorder, OCD, and deep depression. I went from, "how does she do it all" to stuttering, dizzy spells, heart palpitations, irrational fears, and despairing and suicidal thoughts. I was thrust into a season of mental, spiritual, emotional, and physical torment. I battled for my life. My mind raced 24 hours a day.

What if I went crazy? What if I lost it all?

I was terrified.

I had never been here before.

I was at a bible study, and having a volatile day. I was overcome with grief at my condition and overwhelmed by the lie that I could be like this forever. I began begging God to set me free (like I had a million times before), but this was a deep soul cry. Then at that moment, God spoke to my heart, and He said,

"Sarah, do you see? Do you see how my people suffer?" I began to grieve and grieve at the idea that people were suffering from mental and emotional pain like I was. I whispered back "Yes, God, I see" and I knew at that moment that God was lifting the final chains of mental torment off of me so that I could show others the way to freedom too.

Ask anyone who struggles with chronic anxiety how he or she feels when someone advises him or her to "pray it away." All well-intentioned advice but from someone who has overcome a very severe anxiety disorder this is probably the worst advice to give and can keep anxiety suffers in a perpetual cycle of fear. – and my faith-filled friends, I couldn't just pray it away.

Did you know that neurologists have determined that the brain was wired for love? It is scientifically proven that our brains have no pre-set wiring to handle stress and anxiety. When we experience negative emotions, it throws our bodies into chemical chaos because our body and mind are trying to "fix" this strange feeling. It all makes sense.

Of course, we are wired for love, because God is love and He made us LIKE HIM! After working with hundreds of anxiety sufferers, I have discovered that most of the time, the physical, mental, and emotional reaction to a thought is mistrust in the love of God in that area. This was key to my freedom. Whenever I was hit with anxiety I tried everything, I brought my panic to God, I pictured beaches, and breathed deeply, counted to ten, lathered in essential oils but what I needed was to inhale the truth that God fearlessly loved me. When we rattle off panicked prayers like, "make it go away!" our focus is on the feeling of fear, we give it a place in our minds and elevate its power. Instead, don't try to pray it away but rather focus on marinating your mind in love, remembering that – *There is no fear in love. But perfect love drives out fear because fear has to do with punishment. The one who fears is not made perfect in love. 1*St*John 4:18*

When someone reaches out to me with his or her anxiety battle, my first response is never "are you praying enough?" it is always this order: Have you seen your doctor? Are you sleeping enough? Are you exercising? Do you have a support system? Are you in counseling? Do you believe God loves you?

One of the very first things God showed me in my healing journey was that healing needed to take place throughout all of me; my body, my mind, and my spirit. The reason God wants us to focus on all aspects of healing is that they are all interconnected and because God loves ALL OF US! If you have an emotional day you feel fatigued, if you are dealing with a significant sickness or injury, it weighs on your emotions, if you're spiritually dry it makes you heartsick.

I now live with a completely restored, healed, and a renewed mind. Since then, God has placed a fierce determination in me to see people set free from emotional and mental torment like I was. I feel so much compassion when I see others in pain because I know how ravaged their minds are.

Maybe that's you? Perhaps it's not that severe, but your thoughts still hold you back, or maybe you are worse than I was and are on the cusp of giving up. I am here to be a witness and tell you that you can and will live a fearless and joy-filled life! I am still far from virtuous, but I found that spot, nestled right under my Father's wing, a place where there is no fear, no despair, only peace and fullness of joy.

I want to show you how to find that too.

Meeting Sarah at an Edmonton Starbucks – far from her Lethbridge home - was one of those "what-are-the-odds-of-that-happening" experiences. Years later she asked me to endorse her first book, *Fearless In 21 Days*.

For anyone facing depression or anxiety, *Fearless In 21 Days* is your breakthrough in a book.

Sarah E. Ball lives in Cochrane, Alberta, Canada with her husband and five children. Sarah is an author, blogger, speaker, and mental health survivor. She inspires others to live fearlessly by sharing her humour, vulnerability, and faith. Sarah has appeared on several national television programs and has been published in several Christian publications sharing her compelling story from panic to praise. Sarah offers fearless hope to many through her blog, online courses, speaking and book, *Fearless in 21 Days*. Check out her blog saraheball.com.

CHAPTER THREE

Sheila Walsh – It's OK Not To Be OK

God is in control, and he is for us. When we believe that only
then can we let go of what we don't understand and trust God.
~ Sheila Walsh

"I don't often cry at one of my talks. This is very rare for me. Please excuse me."

She wasn't alone with her tears. Men on the Board of the John Cameron Changing Lives Foundation attempted fruitlessly to wipe away their tears. The women Board members had already given up at that task.

Sheila Walsh was in the middle of sharing her story at a private luncheon for the Edmonton-based charity dedicated to raising awareness and removing the stigma of mental health issues.

She was explaining how her father died when she was just five years old. He suffered a cerebral hemorrhage, became partially paralyzed and eventually unable to speak. Soon his personality began to change, growing dark and violent. He threw her mother against a wall and had to be subdued and taken to a psychiatric hospital. Sometime later he escaped, and they found his body in a nearby river. He was just thirty-four years old.

Sheila blamed herself for his behavior.

The last time he looked in her eyes, she saw nothing but pure hatred. She loved her dad, and in her young mind, he could not have been wrong - which meant something terrible had to be in her. After he died, she determined that no one would ever again get close enough to her to see what her dad saw.

The strategy spilled over into her relationship with God. She determined to be the perfect Christian woman, so God would not be disappointed in her. A successful career in music opened the door to co-hosting one of America's most popular Christian TV talk shows. It seemed everyone admired her until one day, and a guest asked her how she was feeling. She was stunned and broke down on the set. Within 24 hours she had left the set of the *700 Club* and was driving north to check herself into a psychiatric hospital. Her TV producers warned her that choice would end her career.

She rehearsed the trauma she felt in the dark as the waves washed around her just off the shoreline of North Carolina. She had stopped her car and waded into the water with the intent of ending her hopeless life.

One day she had been the co-host of the *700 Club*, one of the most popular Christian TV talk shows and the next day she was driving to a hospital to check herself in for treatment of depression. She felt ashamed. How could a Christian in her position be experiencing a mental breakdown? This doesn't happen to people like her. Or it isn't supposed to happen.

What saved her from herself was the memory of her own father's suicide, and the devastation it caused her mom. She couldn't put her mom through the agony of her daughter's death in similar circumstances. She waded back to shore, wiped the tears from her eyes, and forced herself to drive to the hospital.

Sheila is the Scottish girl known as "the encourager" to the over six million women she's met and spoken to around the world. Her purpose is making the Bible practical and sharing her own story of how God met her when she was at her lowest point and lifted her again. She experienced life-long clinical depression and is a champion for those facing mental illness.

She and her husband Barry had just arrived in the city that a former Canadian Prime Minister described as "not the end of the earth, but you can see it from here." They flew from Dallas to College Junction where they spent Friday at Texas A & M for their only son's ring ceremony. They jetted to Detroit, Michigan where Sheila spoke to a thousand women at breakfast. Immediately after the last hug and handshake, they found themselves en route to Edmonton, Alberta arriving late on Saturday night to be ready to speak in three Sunday services at North Pointe Church. And both were genial and concerned about inconveniencing us because of their travel delays.

At the Monday luncheon for the JCCLF, it may have been the hectic schedule or just the emotion of the moment, but Sheila's vulnerability brought everyone to tears. Sheila can make you laugh one moment and have you in tears the next. Whether it's an intimate luncheon or a stadium filled with women, the courage of vulnerability makes her story relatable.

Standing before 5000 women in a west coast auditorium, Sheila Walsh asked the question, "Is there anyone in the audience who has ever attempted suicide or been plagued by suicidal thoughts like I've been? Severe depression? Any kind of mental illness? If so, would you join me in the front?"

I had never shared that part of my journey. Not until now.

I will never forget the next few minutes. Women began to pour to the front of the stage. I stood with tears coming down my cheeks. Some were teens and somewhere in their seventies. There were hundreds and hundreds of them.

Here we all were, and the thought struck me: We were not alone. We were together sharing this holy moment.

"I believe that I shall look upon the goodness of the Lord in the land of the living! Wait for the Lord; be strong, and let your heart take courage; wait for the Lord." Psalm 27:13-14 (ESV)

As I spoke, something became crystal clear. When we try to hide our wounds and scars - all those things we believe make us less lovely - we make fear and shame the stronghold of our lives.

But when we bring our wounds to Jesus, when we out our secrets and shame, we make HIM the stronghold of our lives. He uses our wounds for His purposes. He makes something so beautiful out of our scars. And He wants to do that for you today.

Jesus will make something beautiful from your scars.

If you're like me and you struggle with suicidal thoughts, or if you self-harm in any way, I invite you to join me in a prayer. Copy this onto a card or take a screenshot with your phone. You will have this at hand when the darkness strikes. *You are not alone.*

When the darkness hits, you may feel alone, abandoned, and afraid. I know what despair tastes like, and I see the lie that says it would be better for everyone if you were no longer here. It sounds true, but it comes from the pit of hell. We stand together and declare in Jesus' name that we will live to see the goodness of the Lord in the land of the living.

Lord Jesus Christ, I am broken, but You died so that I might find healing. You were rejected so that I could be fully accepted. I choose life now in Your powerful name. I am Your well-loved child on the days when I feel it and on the days when I don't. I refuse to listen to the lies of the enemy anymore, and I confess with my mouth that in Jesus' name, I will live! Amen.

Amen, my friend.

Sheila loves working worldwide to feed the hungry, give water to the thirsty, provide medical help to the sick, and rescue boys and girls from sex slavery. She most recently traveled to Africa, the Dominican Republic, and Southeast Asia.

She also enjoys being an author she likes to write every day—and has sold more than five million books including *IN THE MIDDLE OF THE MESS, STRENGTH FOR THIS BEAUTIFUL, BROKEN LIFE* and *LOVED BACK TO LIFE.* She is also the co-host of the television program *Life*

Today, airing in the U.S., Canada, Europe, and Australia with over 300 million viewers daily.

Purchase a copy of Sheila's latest book, *Its Ok Not To Be Ok* on her website: TheBraveheartSisterhood.com or Amazon.com.

Sheila Walsh Quotes:

If guilt tells us that we've done something wrong, then shame tells us that we are something wrong. So many people feel isolated, not good enough, defined by the labels they wear rather than the identity they have in Christ. The love of Christ tells us that we're accepted; that we belong.

We live in a culture of quick fixes. We want to feel better, and we want to feel better now. I believe that's why many turn to alcohol and drugs because they want to numb the pain of life. In my life, I have a choice. I can sit with my depression and look at Jesus, or I can sit with Jesus and look at my depression. What I mean by that is I can focus on what's broken and wonder where God is, or I can sit in the companionship of Christ who suffered for us and worship him in the middle of the mess. That gives my pain, meaning and context.

God has promised that whatever you face, you are not alone. He knows your pain. He loves you. And He will bring you through the fire.

If we mistake God's silence for indifference, we are the most miserable of people. If we give up when we no longer understand, we reject His caring, steadfast love and cut ourselves off from our only real hope.

When our dreams seem to go sour or remain unfulfilled, hopelessness can dominate our lives-or we can hold on with open hands, knowing that we have hope because God is faithful.

If depression has been viewed as a taboo subject in the church, then suicide and suicidal thoughts are the darkest secrets of all. Talking about it doesn't make it more real or powerful; it brings it out of the shadows into the light and love of Christ.

My times of silence before God are very important to me now. I put everything else down, every word away, and I am with the Lord. When I'm quiet, life falls into perspective for me. I have a very active mind, and I'm a worrier, but in those moments when I choose to put that away, I rest beside the Shepherd in still places. Why don't you give yourself a gift today? Turn off the television or the car stereo, put down the newspaper or the business plan, and in the quietness, rest for a while beside the Shepherd of your soul.

Suffering is seldom an item on our list of requests to the Lord. But when it crosses our path and we are able by his grace to keep on walking, our lives become messages of hope to the world and the church.

In these uncertain times, I know 100 percent that I can stake my life on the unshakeable, unchanging promises of God!

Can't you tell when you're with someone who's listening? She hears you, really hears you. He hears the sadness in your tone or catches your joy. Be a listener, to music, to life, to others, to God. Life is noisy, but there is music in every heartbeat. God is waiting to bring joy and peace to the confusion of our days.

God's love is a gift that can make you forget yourself at times. The Scottish writer George MacDonald said, "It is the heart that is not yet sure of its God that is afraid to laugh in his presence." God loves us as we are right now! That's one of the things I'm most grateful for. I love the freedom to be myself in God. I pray that a year from now, five years from now, I will be a godlier woman, but I know God won't love me any more than he does right this minute.

CHAPTER FOUR

Joanne Goodwin – Destroying The Stigma of Mental Illness

The difference between guilt and shame is very clear—in theory. We feel guilty for what we do. We feel shame for what we are.
~ Lewis Smedes

Optimism is the faith that leads to achievement. Nothing can be done without hope and confidence.
~ Helen Keller

My therapist said I have acute personality disorder. I was like, "I know, right?"

Once you've met Joanne Goodwin, you can't shake hearing her unforgettable voice in your head. And that's a good thing.

It only takes once, and she's got you for life.

Joanne dispenses medicine for your soul. She's got a double Ph.D. in joy and humor. Across North America, thousands of women attribute their sanity to Joanne.

Her prescriptions have no side effects other than a sore gut from laughing.

She learned their secret the hard way.

After a lifelong battle with mood disorders, depression, bipolar 2 and family crises, cancer became Joanne's most recent opponent. In August 2016, she was diagnosed with stage 3 colorectal cancer. She endured long weeks of radiation, surgery, and chemo.

You correctly guessed if you imagined that she's handling all of this with faith in God.

And a hefty dose of humour.

- - - - -

My mother used to tell me, "Joanne, you don't have to tell everything." It wasn't a problem for me telling people about my depression. The problem was how they reacted.

I shared with one of our church members that I had been diagnosed with depression and was taking anti-depressants, she looked at me and said, "You should just throw the medication down the toilet and trust in Jesus."

What ruined the advice from this individual was that she was wearing prescription glasses herself, so I responded, "Why don't you throw your glasses down the toilet, and we'll do it together."

When I was growing up, I didn't say much about my depression. We were a family that didn't complain. What was I supposed to say to people?

"I'm SO sad."

And they'd say, "Why?"

I didn't have a reason. I just felt sad.

I grew up in a charismatic, emotional type of church, and that's a tough one because they want you to be happy. All. The. Time.

If you say, you're depressed, "Oh, that's so unspiritual."

I didn't know what to do. We'd sing at church, "Happy, happy, happy, happy, happy. Happy are the people whose God is the Lord."

And I'm suicidal.

So I didn't know what to do with it all.

I didn't get diagnosed until I was 40. By then, I was a pastor's wife, I had three little kids, and I was going through these awful depressions. When I felt good, I was very good, and people thought of me as lively and outgoing.

They didn't know that I would disappear for days at a time. I'd be in my room. I couldn't talk. I wondered if I was crazy.

The turning point for me was I did something courageous and made an appointment with a psychiatrist. Pastors' wives aren't supposed to go to a psychiatrist. At least that's why I imagined.

The psychiatrist told me I needed medication. What? I was German. Good. Strong like bull. I can't be depressed. And as a pastor's wife, I wasn't supposed to do drugs to feel good.

But that was my turning point. The medication worked. What a difference. Night and day. I remember saying to my husband, "Does everybody feel like this?" It felt like a miracle.

So much of clinical depression is a bio-chemical imbalance.

One church member told me, "You know that God will keep them in perfect peace whose minds are stayed on Him." That's excellent advice for anyone who can control their thinking. One of the symptoms of depression is the inability to focus. So you can't keep your mind stayed on Jesus. You can't control your thoughts.

It's like saying to someone with Alzheimer's, "Oh stop it. You know who you are."

I was eight months on medication when all hell broke loose in our family. We faced family tragedies that tore us apart for 20 years. Those are stories that would fill another book.

I've learned more about God through the tragedies of my life than any other source. When you suffer, and you see your child suffer, you learn to depend on the grace of God so much. I learned to trust God when everything was out of control.

I've met all kinds of people who are scared, and they have no hope. I've been there.

All I know is life prepares us to get closer to Jesus.

If it were not for the grace of God, I would be dead.

Perspective changes everything. You can get a different view of what you're going through.

I've used humour as medicine. Laughter is a gift from God. While mental illness and cancer are no laughing matters, you still can laugh.

27 Just In Time Lines From Joanne

1. I'm doing 'Angry Yoga' tonight. It's just lying on a mat and eating chocolate as I shout at my thighs.

2. I pointed to two old ladies sitting across the restaurant from us and told my friend, "That's us in 15 years". She said, "That's a mirror."

3. Do you ever wake up, kiss the person sleeping beside you, and feel glad to be alive? I just did, and I won't be allowed on this airline again.

4. Just tried a kids meal at McDonald's. Unfortunately, her dad chased me away before I got any of her fries.

5. After the hospital chemo, I get "chemo take out" for three days. They didn't even ask if I wanted fries with it! Lousy take out place!

6. Always check the height of nearby ceiling fans before giving a toddler a ride on your shoulders. How I learned this rule is not important.

7. I was sobbing and cried, "I can't see you again. I won't let you hurt me like this again!" My trainer sighed. "It was a sit up. You did one sit up!"

8. Just once I'd like someone to call me "ma'am" without having to add "you need to calm down, or we're going to have to ask you to leave."

9. I know you're not supposed to hug the lady giving out samples at Costco, but the sausage she gave me had cheese inside. Cheese. In. Side. Yes.

10. If a woman asks you if she looks fat, it is not okay to say "no." You must also act completely surprised by the question. Jump backward if necessary.

11. I shout "PIZZA'S HERE" so the delivery guy doesn't think I'm eating two pizzas by myself.

12. A cop just pulled me over and asked: "do you know why I stopped you?" I said, "because my FB statuses are so funny?" And then we laughed and laughed and high-fived, and I'm in jail.

13. It's fine to eat a "test" grape in the produce section, but you take one bite of a rotisserie chicken, and it's all, "Ma'am, you need to leave."

14. I went outside without makeup on. A child cried, and I think a bird flew into a window on purpose.

15. If you can't think of a word, say, "I forget the English word for it." That way people will think you're bilingual instead of an idiot.

16. Joe doesn't know this, but for the first three years of our marriage, I thought we were supposed to share a toothbrush.

17. I run from my car to the front door of McDonald's because fitness is a lifestyle.

18. I love Chinese food as much as the next guy, but you'll never convince me a chicken fried this rice.

---

19. Drying out wet fireworks in the oven is not a good idea. I know that now.

---

20. Accidentally went grocery shopping on an empty stomach and now I'm the proud owner of aisle 7.

---

21. Sometimes I pretend I'm picking up lunch for the whole family, even though the KFC workers can see me eating that bucket in their parking lot.

---

22. Current fitness level: my arm gave out while blow drying my hair.

---

23. We've all got that one family member who's an embarrassment. This restraining order suggests my family's settled on me.

---

24. I've always hated math because, in my head, all the word problems sounded like this: The spaghetti envelopes are triangular. Find X.

---

25. I just saw Joe get hit by a snow plow, but in all fairness, I have never driven one of these before.

---

26. I just finished a 5k. It took me four days and was filled with snacks and naps, but at least I finished.

---

27. Yelling at me for warming the towels in the oven is NOT going to get the fire department here any faster!

Joanne is a wife to Joe, mom of three, grandma, recording artist, author, pastor, communicator, and friend. She's proof that a cheerful heart is a good medicine. All of Joanne's experiences paired with her incredible story-telling skills add up to an experience you won't soon forget!

Follow Joanne on her website: joannegoodwin.ca

BOB JONES

CHAPTER FIVE

Vahen King – The Strength of my Weakness

Let your hopes, not your hurts, shape your future.
~ Robert H. Schuller

For the longest time, I doubted my abilities and myself. I just couldn't move forward. I always knew I wanted to do more or be more, but my search to know the cause of what was limiting me took a while.

Finally, I realized that the only thing holding me back was my fear. But what was I afraid of?

Fear of failure? Fear of people's opinions of me? As I continued to search for that root cause of what was continually limiting me, the question never left me: "What am I afraid of?"

In my heart, I knew that I would find the answer.

"God, I'll love and serve You with all of my heart."

That was my honest prayer.

In my first year at Eastern Pentecostal Bible College, I told God that I would go through anything as long as I knew He was with me. I truly believed, "that with God all things were possible." Matthew 19:26

After graduating from Bible College, I received an engagement ring from the love of my life.

The day Vaughan asked me to marry him, I felt like the luckiest girl in the world.

One week to the day after Vaughan proposed, my life took a drastic turn. I experienced excruciating pain in my upper chest and back, and I was rushed to the hospital. As I waited to see the doctor, I remember trying to roll over, but couldn't move my legs. I knew something wasn't right and cried out for the nurse.

When I told her what was happening, she immediately wheeled

me into the emergency ward. Every 15 minutes, they would check my vitals. I was losing feeling and movement so rapidly, that the doctors were scared my lungs would fail, and they would lose me. By evening, I was paralyzed from the chest down, with no use of my right arm.

No one knew what was wrong with me.

I was terrified and overwhelmed with fear. I cried out, "God, I'm so scared!" But at that moment, I felt Him say, "I am with you always." Knowing God was with me, gave me a peace that I cannot explain.

I was subjected to every test you can imagine. A month later, the specialist told me, "Vahen, you have Transverse Myelitis. There is nothing we can do. We are going to send you to a facility where you'll receive full-time care and be dependant on a wheelchair for the rest of your life."

During all the uncertainty surrounding my health, my biggest question was, "Do I still have a fiancé?"

I had to ask Vaughan if he still wanted to marry me. You can imagine my surprise when I heard the words, "Vahen, I love you! God gave you to me, I'm not going to give you back now and say you're not good enough!"

Looking forward to our future together, I ignored the doctor's prognosis, and focused on my rehabilitation, planning our wedding and walking down the aisle.

One year after the doctors said I would never walk again, with my parents on either side of me, I walked the aisle to meet my groom.

Vaughan and I were beginning our life together - a little differently than most young married couples, but we assumed that our biggest problems were behind us.

However, that was just the beginning of the many challenges we'd face as a newlywed couple.

I surrendered all my failures and weaknesses to God, and He said, "I CAN USE THAT." This was **no** overnight operation, but I did have a heart transplant. He has totally transformed my life and my marriage and filled me with so much love and joy! Now He is using it as a platform to showcase His overcoming power.

In what ways do you feel weak or not enough? My challenge to you is this, instead of being ashamed of your weaknesses surrender them fully to God, so He can give you His power.

"My grace is sufficient for you, for my power is made perfect in weakness. Therefore, I will boast all the more gladly about my weaknesses, so that Christ's power may rest on me." 2 Corinthians 12:9

Many times I've been asked, "How do you do it?" "How do you get the strength to keep going?" "Do you not have any fear?" My response would always be, "Of course I still have fear, but my relationship with God helps me go farther. It gives me the strength to "push past" what it "feels like" and not let fear hold me back."

Bruce H. Wilkinson said it best,

"People often feel that because they are afraid of something, they do not have the courage to conquer it. However, courage is not the absence of fear: rather, it's choosing to act in spite of fear."

At the beginning of 2015, I felt that this year would be the year of pushing past even more of my fears. I had entered the season of "being more." As I began embracing this, the results have become more than I ever expected.

I have been in a wheelchair since 1999 due to a medical condition called Transverse Myelitis. Now, after 17 years, I have just taken my first steps unassisted! My dreams of doing and being more are becoming more of a reality than I ever thought possible.

Through all the highs and lows, I am thrilled to share my journey with the world around me. I have learned from my own experience that you don't actually have the power to control your life.

The sudden onslaught of a paralyzing medical condition was a significant contradiction to my "own power." In my recovery process, there definitely was a role I had to play. However, as I rediscovered my relationship with God, He showed me that I can only go so far in my own strength. With Him, I could go farther than I ever hoped or imagined if I let go of my fear.

Every day I had to make tough choices, and the way I responded to my choices determined whether or not I could go farther. My new perspective allows me to look ahead with great expectations. I am thankful to God for all my happiness and success. It is because of Him, I am choosing courage and going farther. Thank you for taking this journey with me.

I have chosen to put my name in Philippians 1: 6 "... being confident of this very thing, that He who has begun a good work in me will complete it until the day of Jesus Christ."

In 2017, Vahen was crowned the first ever Miss Wheelchair Canada, and won Miss Kindness on the international stage. Vahen has used her journey, to ignite hearts with hope and to make a difference, which was what fueled her vision to create a non-profit charity "Going Farther."

If you want to learn more of how Vahen can inspire you, go to www.goingfarther.org, or purchase her book, *Going Farther: Experience the Power and Love of God That Turns Tragedy Into Triumph* on Amazon.ca.

CHAPTER SIX

Wendy Edey – The Monster of Grief

Hope begins in the dark, the stubborn hope that if you just
show up and try to do the right thing, the dawn will come. You
wait and watch and work: You don't give up.
~ Anne Lamott

Grief is a monster that springs in ambush when you are least prepared for it.

It squeezes the life out of you until you can barely breathe. At least that's what I'm noticing about grief these days. It's a recent discovery. I've viewed it differently in the past.

Monsters were distinctly absent from my previous encounters with grief. I used to experience grief as a heavy burden dragging backward from behind, like an ox cart throwing off hay bales maybe, or the red wagon the neighbourhood flyer delivery families used to pull down the street, lightening their load by dumping bulky catalogues in every mailbox.

Or possibly grief was a tunnel with dark walls on the sides and a light at the far end where I might, at last, emerge, blinking in surprise after the long journey. These things I imagined in my days of smaller griefs.

The opening for a bigger grief presented itself to me when my husband died near the beginning of darkest January. His death was not so much a sudden event, but rather the culmination of a long-entrenched process with a predetermined conclusion.

Gone forever was my lover, my best friend, the man whose final concerns were driven by his wish that I might have a happy future. There I was, a widow after 45 years of a happy marriage, waiting for the burden of grief to drag me back or the tunnel to close me in. But where was the burden? Where was the tunnel. Where was the sadness?

I waited for the grief to happen.

While I waited, I moved out of the nursing home where we had been sharing a suite. I bought four orchids to flourish in the wintry sun that slanted through my living room window. I sang as I cleaned my kitchen. I played Bridge with good friends and exercised at the YMCA.

Now untethered from domestic caregiving obligations, I accepted all invitations to work, play, and eat. But where was the burden? Where was the tunnel? Could the process of grieving really be dispensed with so easily?

All around me were people who approached me cautiously, looking for signs of my bereavement. I told them all that I was doing fine. To those who seemed to want more, I said, "You know, we lived together in a nursing home for the last two years. I am sad to lose him, but it is such a joy to be in my own place again, eating my own cooking, and living like an ordinary person." It hardly seemed an adequate tribute. But I could offer no better accounting than that.

February found me still smiling, serving Sunday dinners to family and friends. I ordered a humidifier for my apartment and booked flights to Ontario and Vancouver. Grieving in a recognizable configuration still had not begun.

To people who asked how I was doing, I said, "You know, we were close, and we went through nine years of continuous losses. At first, he couldn't skate, and then he couldn't take long walks. Then he couldn't keep working and then he had to give up driving. Eventually, he couldn't operate the TV remote or feed himself. We mourned all those losses together. So I guess maybe my mourning was pretty much done by the time he died."

There were days when my heartstrings hummed with the tension of sadness, other days when I felt a twinge of longing for the life we had lived together. I greeted these symptoms with some relief. Still, it didn't seem quite enough. "This is grief," I said to myself, "And it is not so bad. Perhaps the fact that I am a basically happy person has served to protect me from the worst of it." February, however, is a short month.

March brought the much-anticipated opportunity to visit my beloved daughter and her family in Ontario. Ontario hadn't seemed so far away when David was ill. Our daughter had made it her mission to be with us as often as possible. Now it was my turn to go to her.

With joyful enthusiasm, I packed a small bag. It had been a long time since I had been free to travel. I smiled all the way to the airport, joked my way through security and happily read a novel while we passed over the prairies and Northern Ontario.

It wasn't until the flight attendant announced the beginning of our descent that the monster first came for me. One minute I was fine. The next minute I wasn't fine at all. My chest was tight. My throat was clogged. My body was acting beyond my control, sobs were shaking my shoulders, and tears were pouring down my cheeks. I surrendered in bewilderment.

At that particular moment, there was no reason to be sad, and I was sadder than I had ever been.

Just across the tarmac, on the other side of a door, three little blue-eyed blonds were tugging at their mother wondering; "When is Granny coming out?" I had longed to embrace them. Yet now, at the moment when this could be, my thoughts had retreated to a point back in history, the times when we used to talk about the grandchildren we would have someday.

David and I were going to take those children camping. We were going to take them to the zoo. We were going to read to them together and take them to the library. Now David was not here for those things.

I was still wiping my nose when I exited the airplane. Never had I felt more alone.

Waiting to hug me, as I crossed the threshold, were the bouncing apples of my eye, the delights of my heart. So bereft was I that it took all the discipline I could muster to greet them with the enthusiasm I would have felt an hour earlier. Had it been even a little bit possible, I might have curled up on the floor of the arrivals area, clutching my knees to my heaving breast.

"Fake it till you make it," I said to myself.

Faking it was the best I could do at the time. Fortunately, I would be with them for six days—time enough to restore my equilibrium. Later, with only the memory of the emptiness to show for my sudden outburst, I patted myself on the back. "Now you have experienced grief," I said. "You got through it all right. Return to the process of building a satisfying life."

So I bought a new piano and played it every morning. I registered at a seniors centre and joined a writing club. I chose spring bulbs and pots of pansies to grow on my balcony. March went out like a lamb.

April brought me a plugged ear that required the attention of a doctor. I hadn't seen this doctor since I left the nursing home. He used to come to our suite on Fridays. We'd worked closely together, giving the best care we could for David. Somehow we'd managed to maintain a cheery disposition and a stiff upper lip in the face of so much suffering and helplessness.

A plugged ear is much easier to fix than a neuro-degenerative illness. In the face of such a simple task, I looked forward to telling him about my new piano, my plans for spring, the flowers I was growing. But as soon as he asked me how I was doing, the monster came out of nowhere and nailed me to the chair. I felt the tightening of my chest, and my face refused to smile. I took a deep breath to calm myself. Clearly, I was not going to be able to tell him about the new piano or the flowers.

Acting on its own, with no permission from me, my mouth blurted, "Just sitting here with you is giving me PTSD."

"Really?" he asked in surprise.

"Really," I said, for now, I was back in the nursing home, trying to live one day at a time, trying not to wish away the together time that remained for David and me, wishing I could do more for him, wishing I could do it better.

"That's funny," the doctor said. "Being here with you isn't giving me PTSD."
This, I knew, was an invitation to let it go. The old familiar me would have laughed. The old familiar me would have told him about the pansies and the family dinners on Sundays. But with the monster gripping my neck, all I could manage to say was: "I think it's only my left ear, but you can check the right one."
And when I got home, clear-eared and heart-broken, I lay on my bed for hours, hugging my knees to my heaving breast. "Move past it," I said to myself. "Forget the monster and go on with your life. Or maybe learn to keep an eye out, so it's not such a shock when it springs."

On my phone was a text from Alayne, inviting me to join her on a trip to the farmers' market. Alayne was a friend of David's, then later a friend of mine by association. In those last couple of years, she continued to visit, came in the last few weeks knowing David would be unable to speak. I accepted her offer with trepidation, knowing myself to be vulnerable in a way I had not been before.

If ever there was a good place for a monster to lie in wait, then that place was surely the farmers' market, the very one where David and I had spent many joyful Saturday mornings in years gone by. We went so often that the vendors noticed our absences and asked why we'd been away. All my senses were on alert, waiting for the ambush that never came.

This visit to the market was not quite like the others. None of the vendors remembered me. I'd been away that long. Nobody wondered how I was doing. With a tremulous awakening of confidence, I picked up an opulent hydrangea, then a fragrant Easter lily. I snatched up a jar of my favourite Sauerkraut and added a bag of carrots. Into the mix, I threw a package of jerk chicken sausages, fresh pita, hummus, and finally, a chocolate treat made from ground up crickets that I thought I'd take to entertain the unsuspecting snackers at the bridge club.

Smiling triumphantly in my kitchen as I unpacked the load, I said, "Aha Monster. I fooled you, didn't I? You thought you'd scare me away from the farmers' market, and I went anyway."

But even as I said it, I began to suspect that this grief, which was neither a burden to be slowly unloaded, nor a tunnel with a light at the end, was a smarter-than-average monster.

Smarter-than-average monsters are too smart to ambush you when you're ready for them. They know enough to wait until you aren't.

With that in mind, as I plan my second trip to Ontario, I am hoping the monster never strikes twice in the same place.

Insights to Healing After Loss:

Don't let others set a timetable for you to be over your loss.

Don't allow yourself to set a timetable to live a new normal.

There is no normal, and grief is not something you get over. Grief is something you go through. It becomes a part of the fabric of your life. The funeral is over, the flowers have long faded, you've eaten the leftovers from the last of the casseroles brought to you by caring friends and neighbours, and you discover that grief will sneak up on you at the least expected time. It may manifest in a flood of unexpected tears during a family celebration or awkward laughter at a sombre occasion because a memory of your loved one came to mind.

North Americans don't do well with grieving.

We cry in secret.

We stuff our sorrow.

We rush our mourning.

Grief lasts as long as it lasts.

Time doesn't heal – grieving does.

Grieving is moving forward, and it will be at your pace. Don't let anyone rush you. After all, you're learning to run with a limp.

"If you haven't already, you will lose someone you can't live without...and your heart will be badly broken, and the bad news is that you will never completely get over the loss of a beloved person. But this is also the good news. They will live forever, in your broken heart that doesn't seal back up. And you come through. It's like having a broken leg that never heals perfectly – that still hurts when the weather is cold. You learn to run with a limp." Anne Lamott

Comfort comes to those who mourn. It is never too late to mourn. Even if your loss occurred years or decades ago, there is healing in mourning now.

Healing occurs when people have the opportunity to talk about their grief experiences and hear others who are dealing with similar heartache. Grief Share is a healthy environment for mourning. Weekly group sessions are offered in many churches and some funeral homes. They are designed to follow the viewing of a video, allowing an opportunity for discussion of the content, and a time of personal sharing for group members.

The support group discussion time, led by empathetic facilitators, will allow people to share their feelings and experiences. You'll experience an atmosphere of care and concern with solid, reliable teaching and support.

- - - - -

Wendy Edey **is** the former Director of Counselling, "Hope Studies Central" at the University of Alberta, in Edmonton, Alberta.

Since 1995, Wendy – a psychologist – has practiced and taught the intentional integration of hope strategies into counselling for people facing illness and complex problems.

Her pioneering work in the development of hope-focused language earned the Canadian Counselling Association Award for practice excellence and the University of Alberta Alumni Award for excellence in achievement.

Wendy is known by her friends as *"The Hope Lady."*

Wendy writes about things that turned out better than expected and impossible things that became possible. She shares about hoping, coping, and moping in stories about disability, aging, caregiving, and child development.

Wendy is blind, but she has crystal clear vision of what's essential in life.

"I learned to read and write Braille when I was ten years old. I learned by correspondence from Doris Goetz, the CNIB Home Teacher, who visited me exactly three times, bringing a new book each time she came. It took me five months to learn the alphabet and all the contractions. It wouldn't have taken so long had it not been for the fact that Doris wouldn't give me the next book in the Braille Series until she came to visit."

Wendy says, "Put two ideas into a jar, shake well, open the jar, and see what you have. Will it be humor, some fabulous new invention, or two separate ideas—shaken, but not combined?"

"I have built a career on the two-idea mixing concept: What do you get when you combine hope with getting old, with offender treatment, with having Parkinson's Disease, with parenting a child with disabilities? What do you get when you combine hope with being a cancer physician, a corporate CEO, a refugee?"

Wendy helps people who have been shaken up by life to combine hope and their circumstance to live life to its fullest.

Wendy says:

Troubled people call on hope,
Thinking nothing short of magic can help them now.

They say: "I am the sum of my experience."
Hope says: "Yes, that plus your hopes for the future."

They say: "What if I don't have any hopes for the future?"
Hope says: "Then we'll find some."

They say: "Where will we find them if no hopes are there?"
Hope says: "We'll find them in your past experience added to the past experience of others, added to the future you haven't explored yet."

"Past experience has tied you in knots," says Hope. "Hold on to me as we work at the loosening."

Then they, with surprising frequency, say: "Okay."

And before they have time to think about it, they are working the knots, making room for hope to perform the magic.

Read more from Wendy at THE HOPE LADY at:

thehopelady.blogspot.com.

CHAPTER SEVEN

Katelyn Murray – My Beaded Journey

The central struggle of parenthood is to let our hopes for our
children outweigh our fears.
~ Ellen Goodman

Katelyn Murray, or as her soccer teammates in St Albert know her, Kate, was in Calgary for a weekend shopping trip with her mom and sister in January 2016. Friday evening, Kate wasn't feeling very well. It seemed nothing that some TLC and sleep wouldn't take care of. When her discomfort persisted into the early morning hours, her mom, Amanda, drove her to Emergency at the Alberta Children's Hospital for attention.

Mom suspected that Kate had a severe case of the flu. She was stunned when doctors shared their diagnosis.

"Leukemia!?"
The room spun.

The very sound of the word was devastating. In one instant, the Murrays' whole world changed. The doctor's reassuring words sounded a million miles away. "It's a good thing we diagnosed this early. We can begin treatment right away."

Overnight, Kate went from a competitive soccer player to a fearless cancer fighter. Isolation, IV's, anesthetics, NPO, surgery, IVAD port, lumbar puncture, bone marrow biopsies, chemotherapies, counts and protocols, anti-nausea, and pain medications were so many new things to learn during her first eleven days of treatment in Calgary. She was then released from the hospital to return home for extended treatment at the Stollery Children's Hospital in Edmonton.

Like all parents with kids fighting cancer, Amanda became an overnight expert on Kate's diagnosis. From the attending physicians and what she read, Amanda was assured leukemia is a cancer that can be cured because it's a disease of the blood. Early diagnosis and treatment bode well for children like Kate.

However, Kate's diagnosis suddenly turned from under control to chaos. Doctors informed the Murrays the results from further tests indicated Kate had a rare form of leukemia. Rare as in one-in-a-100,000 kind of rare. Kate would require a change in her treatments, a more extended period of treatment, and a lower percentage of success.

Amanda called and requested prayer for Kate.

"We're new to North Pointe, Pastor Bob. You haven't met us before. Would you have time?"

No question about it.

"May I come to your home?"
Our youth pastor, Jeremy Gifford, and I made plans to meet Kate for prayer and some creative TLC.

Collecting Coke memorabilia from all over the world is one of my addictions. A truck on my bookcase made from a Coke can called Kate's name. It has a cyan-colored stick shift – perfect for Kate because her favourite color is cyan.

Shareen Baker, our graphic artist, designed a greeting card heavy on cyan. A cyan-colored gift bag with cyan-colored filler made our get-well gift complete.

On the way to the Murray's home, we made quick stops at Booster Juice for Kate's favourite drink - a "Himalayan Twist" - and 7-11 for some Beef Jerky. The chemo treatments gave Kate a craving for "beef."

Kate was snuggled up in a blanket on a couch in the living room. Her smile told us the Twist tasted pretty good. The jerky would wait for another day. Who knew that trucks – especially ones with cyan-colored stickshifts - were Kate's favourite vehicle? We were off to a good start.

Her family, including Grampa and the family's dogs, gathered around for what would be the first of many prayer times.

Within a few days, Kate collected the first of many decorative beads she would receive from Kids With Cancer. The organization calls treatments for cancer in children their *Beaded Journey*. A unique bead was crafted for each blood transfusion, spinal tap, chemo treatment, and other treatments. Kate's chain would grow to over thirty-five feet in no time. By the end of March, her hair began falling out quickly, and it was itchy. Time to go bald. She spent most of her time in the hospital from February to July. By the end of April, she was giving herself twice daily injections and de-accessing her IVAD.

Kate decided to turn her cancer experience into a way of serving God. She strongly felt that God was going to use her cancer to speak into the lives of others. In keeping with that impression, she chose to get baptized in water as a public declaration of her faith in Jesus and her desire to shine for him through her cancer journey. Water baptism is a public step that followers of Jesus take as a witness to their death to self and new life in God. A few days after her first chemo treatment, Kate was baptized before a cheering crowd at North Pointe.

Over the next two years, Kate found herself more than once at death's door. Only the mercy of God through the quick and efficient work of medical attendants saved her life. Each incident drained a little more energy and hope out of the Murrays. Mom and dad would take turns overnighting in Kate's room. In a real way, the prayers of others sustained them. Kate had one year and two months of intensive chemotherapy treatments. During her ten intensive rounds of treatment, she had 420 oral chemotherapy doses, 101 IV chemotherapy doses, and 14 spinal chemotherapy doses. She had severe side effects to her intensive treatment and needed 50 blood transfusions, nine ultrasounds, four CAT scans, four GFR's, six ECG's, and six echocardiograms. She felt perpetually exhausted

We created *The Breakfast Club*. Every day for almost two years, people fasted from 12:00am – 12:00pm and prayed for Kate. For those of the opinion that prayer doesn't make a difference, I can tell you that it made a difference in those who prayed. And Kate will say it made a difference in her.

Doctors believed that the chemo treatments had compromised her bone structure, and her legs would not be able to carry her weight for strenuous physical activity – like soccer. Kate's dream was to play internationally on the Canadian Women's soccer team. Was her dream dead? Kate prayed. Others prayed. It was excellent news when she was informed that her bones looked good to go.

Celebs like Connor McDavid, Brett Kissel and members of the Edmonton Eskimo Football club made time to visit the Stollery, sign autographs and encourage kids. The nursing staff at the Stollery became a second family to the Murrays.

Kate was always willing to give back. She was chosen as the Kids With Cancer spokesperson in 2017 and delivered her inspiring story at numerous fundraising events. Kate's sense of humor and practical way of sharing her life and death experiences with cancer won the hearts of hearers. After her talk at the Annual Kids With Cancer gala, a record-setting amount of donations were made.

On Sunday, February 4, 2018 (World Cancer Day), Kate told her story and rang her "end-of-treatment-bell" at North Pointe Church. Kate Murray is one tough teen.

She hosted a party that afternoon in North Pointe's gym for everyone who supported her. A ginormous cake and beverages along with a photo collage of Kate and a banner signed by well-wishers, including Alberta's own Brett Kissel, lined the tables.

Kate told those assembled:

"If you can believe it, I used to be a normal kid. I've always been short for my age, but nothing like I am now. I haven't grown at all because of my chemo treatments over the past two years.

At one time, my doctors told me my bones would not support my weight, and I could never play soccer again. That was devastating. My dream was to play on Canada's Olympic soccer team."

What a surprise in November 2017 when my doctor told me that it looked like my bones were now A-OK to go.

I'm starting to get back into soccer, and my dream is alive again. Being much shorter and lighter than the other players, I tend to get hurt more often. Because I get hurt, some people see me as weak. But if they knew that it's a miracle that I am still alive and playing the game, I think they would realize I am actually tough.

The cancer started all this in the first place, but it was the treatment that made me sick.

* *My kidneys shut down for twenty-five days.*
* *I got a blood clot on my port that required me to take blood thinners.*
* *A nose tube was inserted into my stomach. That may not sound too horrible, but it gave me ulcers in my throat and stomach. I remember every detail of it.*
* *My liver was compromised.*
* *My treatments left me forgetful and disoriented.*
* *I developed drop foot. I couldn't lift my feet.*
* *My nerves were damaged and my brain couldn't talk to some parts of my body.*
* *When I was really sick, even getting out of my bed and walking around the fish tank in my unit was a lot of effort.*
* *My potassium levels dropped. That always caused muscle cramping. Your heart is a muscle. My heart was compromised more than once.*

* *I suffered blood poisoning and was on the edge of septic shock. ICU doctors worked for eight hours to stabilize me.*
* *I had bone fractures and bladder infections.*

One thing that made me mad during my treatments. My friends would ask me if I was coming to school. When I told them I couldn't because of my cancer, they would reply, "You are so lucky."

I want everyone to know that missing school, meeting someone special, going to an Oilers game, or having some cool experiences are not worth it. I would rather have lived a normal healthy life than had two years of being near death.

But what these experiences did for me was to feel loved and not forgotten about. They gave me a break from the battle and made me feel stronger. Moving forward, I will have monthly appointments, blood tests, and other tests. I am in remission and will be considered for the next five years. After five years, the doctors will call me cured.

It's hard to know how to help someone sick. Then once you know, you're never sure if you are doing the right thing.

Thank you for everything you've done for me."

In April 2018 Kate was back on the soccer pitch fearlessly defending her portion of the turf. She plays a lot taller than her stature should allow. Few, if any of her opponents, knew of her battles with cancer but they sure felt her competitive drive.

Now Kate's ready for a new chapter in her life. God has written her life story. What blessings are ahead?

Thank you, Kate, for everything you've done for us.

BOB JONES

CHAPTER EIGHT

Kristen Fersovitch – Still I Will Sing

Hope ... is not a feeling; it is something you do.
~ Katherine Paterson

"It's been a while since I've seen you. I hope summer has been treating you great."

The message from Kristen hit my inbox on Tuesday, August 16, 2011, at 6:09pm.

Anyways the reason for my email is I have a prayer request. Today was my first six-month checkup since my kidney surgery, and I fully expected them to say, "looks great!" and send me on my way; however, that wasn't the case.

They saw that my right kidney had some swollen lymph nodes on it and want to look into it further. The radiologist told me his report and recommendation would be at my Doctor's by tomorrow, as he wants to compare today's ultrasound findings to previous ultrasounds (thinking that maybe these swollen nodes may have always been there).

Pastor Bob, I am so frustrated I feel like I've reached my wits end with everything we have been through in the last 3½ yrs. It seems like the storm is never gonna end.

I know God is in this, I know he has a plan... But it's really hard to keep my head up this time. And I feel like I need to - having a positive attitude is so good for a person... But I don't know.

I'm just frustrated.

Things aren't good. The lymph nodes are massive. There are three, and the largest one measures four cm, the second is two cm. and the third is smaller than that.
They are probably going to be treating it as reoccurring cancer.

I'm scared and yet, not.

When I press on the right side of my abdomen right by my rib cage, I can feel a hard lump. And it hurts.

Please pray that all will be well. And even if they do say the worst (cancer has spread to your lymph nodes) that all parties involved can be absolutely on top of everything.

You know I will fight whatever comes head on, but I feel I need an army of prayer behind me.

I first met Kristen Miller Fersovitch when she was eight-years-old as her pastor. Twenty-one years later, she was now a firefighter's wife and mom to three pre-schoolers. A week after sending her email, it was Kristen at the other end of a phone call. *"Pastor Bob, can I sing a song this Sunday?"*

In spite of a prognosis of death, she wanted to worship. The song that came to her mind says it all:

"When hope is lost, I'll call you Saviour
When pain surrounds, I'll call you healer
When silence falls, you'll be the song within my heart
I will praise you, I will praise you
When the tears fall, still I will sing to you
I will praise you, Jesus praise you
Through the suffering still, I will sing."
(When Tears Fall, Tim Hughes)

The day after sharing her story and song at North Pointe she wrote,

Thank you SO MUCH for letting Kennedy (her sister) and I sing on Sunday. I know it was my idea (well kind of) I'm telling you in all honesty, as I was sitting in the front row waiting to get called up I couldn't help but think " WHO'S INSANE IDEA WAS THIS!!!??? I DON'T WANT TO DO THIS!!!"

But I am glad I did, and I know the purpose for it.

After a lot of prayer, we really felt that God was leading us towards a

therapy called Gerson Therapy. Basically, this therapy is all about rebuilding your immune system to fight cancer naturally. Mike and I have cut out salt, sugar, meat & dairy and are now consuming only fresh organic fruits and vegetables. There is also a lot of juicing done throughout the day and taking a lot of supplements too.

My day pretty much looks like this:

8am- 8oz Orange Juice & Oatmeal
9:00 Green Juice (made of Green Swiss chard, Romain Lettuce, Red Cabbage, Red Lettuce, Beet tops, green pepper, granny smith apple)
9:30 Carrot/ Apple Juice
10:00 Carrot/ Apple juice
11:00 Carrot Juice
12:00 Green Juice
1:00 Carrot/ Apple + Lunch (which is usually a special soup + Salad, and Veggies)
2:00 Green Juice
3:00 Carrot Juice
4:00 Carrot Juice
5:00 Carrot Apple Juice
6:00 Green Juice
7:00 Carrot Apple Juice

All of these juices are made fresh every hour, and I can eat as many fruits and veggies as needed.

Today is day six of this whole ordeal, and it's been trying at times that's for sure. It takes 30 - 40 hours a week to do (A FULL-TIME JOB!) and those 5-6 hours of the day are spent in the kitchen (preparing and cutting veggies & making juice)

It's just so frustrating because everything convenient about food in today's world is totally off limits for us! Like EVERYTHING! I walked through Costco (another favourite place of mine) and realized that I can't consume one thing in that ENTIRE building!!!

So...I was talking to God about this and telling him how sad I was that I couldn't just go to a buffet like everyone else (I don't even like buffet's, to begin with...but whatever) and this thought came to my mind.

"Kristen, you can't go to a food buffet because you feel like God has lead you and asked you to do Gerson Therapy. Isn't that just like following Jesus?"As a follower of him, you can't go, or you've been asked not to partake in "Life Buffets" either. You can't go partying or doing any of the things that the world can do. He has called us to live a different life.

Well, that put me in my place. I wasn't impressed...but it made complete sense, and I knew it was right.

Oh, and I have something else that I wanted to ask you. Something has been on my mind for a while.

Ever since this whole thing has started, I feel like God has been giving me little seeds of hope to cling too as I walk through this with him.

I think I mentioned to you the time when I saw an elderly couple walking holding hands and I thought to myself "that's supposed to be Mike and me one day," and then in the corner of my heart I felt an "it will be" and I was filled with peace and confidence.

Another time when I was having my bone scan at the U of A hospital I was laying on the table and just singing worship songs in my heart and praying (the scan takes about 45mins) and at one point I felt the spirit so heavy and I was praying in tongues and the thought " You will be the prayer warrior for your grandchildren that your grandma Mast was for you" came to me.

And I was so filled with emotion and started crying right in the middle of my scan.

And then this morning I was feeling horrible that my mom and dad have had the boys for the past week and will have them this week too (just so we can get our schedule figured out) and Beckett is supposed to be going to a little preschool class we signed him up for. He missed last week and is missing this week, and I just felt so bad I was feeling so frustrated that this stupid ordeal is affecting EVERYTHING! Even my desire to see Beckett go and play with other little kids. And then I felt "Kristen he is missing a few days of pre-school now so that you can beat this and see him graduate one day."

Sunday, September 4, 2011, Kristen shared her story with vulnerability and courage as a featured part of North Pointe's two services. She sang with all her heart and faith. It was one of those unforgettable moments in which time stood still.

We prayed for Kristen that morning. We believed God to heal her. People kept praying and supporting her over the next 25 months. She passed away on October 4, 2013.

Holding yourself together when everyone else would understand if you fell apart - that's a real strength.

Kristen Fersovitch was one of the strongest women I know. She was at her best when life was at it's worst.

She persevered in spite of cancer, pain, and fear.

Kristen finished her race.

She is still singing.

Kristen changed my life, as well as her family, friends, fans, and strangers. Six years after her passing, we still have our unanswered questions, grief, and the most profound sense of loss. And we have her words.

"God is BIG. Bigger than anything that would try to overcome you or your family. I have come to know God as a provider, sustainer, giver of joy, and peace and so much more...and I am currently on a journey that is leading me to know him as my healer.But let's say I didn't get healed - what if I

died? Would that mean that he wasn't God? No, not at all. We all are going to die; we are not invincible; we are human; we all make mistakes; we all fall short. But there is a God of grace and mercy who made you...so he could love you. He loved you so much that he sent his son Jesus to die for you. For me.

My life is preserved by Jesus because he died for me because I accepted him as my Lord and Savior. He is the giver of life...ETERNAL Life...so when my time here on earth is done, I get to live in eternity with God. THAT is what gets me through each day. That is what sustains and brings peace and joy.

Lord, I trust you. I believe."

There was a full house at Millwoods Assembly for her funeral service on October 10, 2013. Live streaming brought total viewership into the thousands, and there were many more who mourned her loss. CTV Edmonton aired a portion of the service on the 6 o'clock news. Carrie Doll, a CTV news anchor, shared a tribute at the ceremony and spoke for all who were touched by Kristen's life.

Have you ever met someone in life and thought, there is a reason I am meeting this person? It's as if you had something to learn from them, they had something to teach you, but you had no idea what it was.

This is how I felt when I met Kristen. She was beautiful and real, and funny and goofy and graceful and incredibly talented.

But it was her presence, and her spirit, that was larger than life. I wanted to be around her, soak up her aura, I wanted to learn from her.

It was in December 2011. That's where I first heard the name Kristen Fersovitch. My dear friend John Cameron told me he was writing a song, with one of the most amazing people he had ever met. Her name was Kristen. She had 3 children, she was going to sing in the tree, and she was battling terminal cancer. He told me she had changed his life and would impact countless others.

I was intrigued. I wanted to know who this person was, that John had spoken so highly of.

So, a week before the 2011 edition of the Edmonton Singing Christmas Tree opened, CTV News decided to do a story about the Tree, and the young lady more and more people were talking about. Amanda Anderson from CTV News was our reporter. She's a hard-nosed journalist who has covered it all. But apparently not quite all, because when she came back to the newsroom that afternoon after interviewing Kristen, her eyes were red and swollen, and she stopped by my desk and simply said, "I've never met anyone like her, come with me, you need to see this."

She played the interview and the video of John and Kristen singing, and the newsroom fell silent. There was magic and power in Kristen's presence and in her voice. And that was only the beginning. Because when Kristen took center stage at the Singing Christmas Tree to share her story, no one was quite prepared for what she was about to share, and the emotions she was about to evoke in everyone who heard her story. Her message was raw and truthful and painful to listen to. She melted our hearts when she shared pictures of her husband Mike and her three beautiful boys, and she broke our hearts when she told us how sick she really was. And just when you felt you could bear no more, she started to sing. Her voice was pure and powerful, and she used phrases like "There's joy inside of you, something you cannot hide. It brings you hope, it brings you peace. It will come and change your life, though your heart may be broken and you world may seem destroyed. It's Christmas Time, and you can find joy."

What???

Joy — When cancer is tearing you apart?

Joy — When the doctors tell you it's terminal?

Joy — When you look into the faces of your three young children and know you may not be around to see them go to school, see them grow up, see them fall in love?

I stood backstage, and I was frozen, and like every other person in that audience, I cried. I cried for Kristen, for her husband and boys, and their future. For her Mom and Dad and for her sister Kennedy, for the future, this tight-knit family had to face.

And I cried because of all the things she forced me to think about.

What is living really all about? How do you live a life of joy when your world is falling apart?

But she didn't see it that way. She stood on the stage, and she sang her heart out, and as she did, she inspired everyone around her with her remarkable courage. She challenged us to live the best life we can in the face of tragedy, in the face of despair. Not by "telling" us to but by leading by example. She was Joy. And if she can choose it, in light of every challenge she was facing, the message is, all of us can.

And the message resonated with everyone who saw her and everyone who heard about her story. Her kindness and positivity were palpable. You could feel it. She made you feel fortunate and grateful for everything you had in your life. And whether you got to meet her or not, you were motivated to be a "better person.

After the Singing Christmas Tree wrapped for the year, the emails started to pour in. I received countless messages and phone calls and was stopped on the street by people wanting to know "how Kristen was." People had connected with her, she had made an impact. They would follow up those questions with this comment "it was the most powerful performance I have ever seen, I will never forget her. I have never cried so hard, and have been inspired so much all at the same time.

And so I brought her on CTV News, and we talked about the experience, and her humility shone through. She was so taken aback when I called her and asked for the interview. "Why?" She asked. "Why would people want to hear from me? I'm just a big goof." And there lies the beauty of Kristen

Fersovitch, and the power of her spirit. She moved us; she challenged us, without ever saying the words, without offering a piece of advice. She just lived it.

And she lived it for the next year, against all the odds. And whenever you asked her where she got her strength from the answer was very clear. Her faith. It carried her through the darkest times and the most insurmountable challenges and brought her back to the Singing Christmas Tree stage in 2012. And she did it when her health had really taken a turn for the worse.

When she showed up for the Tree, she was clearly in pain, although you'd never hear that from her. She had just finished an intense round of chemotherapy and radiation. She had lost a lot of her hair. So, she wore a wig and made a headband, the most fashionable accessory that year. Her chest was burnt from radiation, and the tumor in that area was painfully obvious. She knew it but wasn't phased by it. Instead, she talked about it with a sense of humor. So she came into my dressing room one night before the show wearing a cute little V-neck t-shirt and said, "look at this thing, auugggghhh, crazy thing, it's so itchy. Oh well, nothing a little high necked dress won't fix." Then we'd sit and talk like girlfriends; she'd try on my shoes, look at my clothes. We'd talk fashion, music and kids and life. When I asked what it was like to share the stage with Rubban Studdard, she said the guy can sing, he just can't remember the words!" When I asked her if she was going to wear her awesome Christian Louboutin shoes this year, she said her feet couldn't take it, kicked off her shoes and went barefoot on stage. And at the end of the night when we were all exhausted, she still found the strength to go to the after show receptions, take pictures, meet people and spread the love. And she did 5 sold out shows because people wanted to see Kristen Fersovitch.

How fitting it was that the theme of the show that year was "The Perfect Gift" because that's what Kristen gave all of us by coming back to that stage and singing one last time.

And as the song goes she wasn't scared to face her fears, she wasn't scared to spread her wings, she didn't mind that we shared her tears, because she taught us love is everything.

We saw it on stage, and we felt it as she gave people she didn't know and us the perfect gift.

On one of the last nights that Kristen performed, I was standing backstage with her Mom and Dad. I looked over at them, and tears were streaming down her Dad's face. I said to him, "You must be so proud." He said, "You know, Carrie, just grateful, grateful for all the time we had with her."

Dave and Kathy, Kennedy, Mike, Lincoln, Tayven and Beckket, thank you for sharing your daughter, your sister, your wife and your mommy with all of us. We too are grateful for everything Kristen taught us and for all the memories we have of her. I now know why the rest of our community and I were supposed to meet her and get to know Kristen Fersovitch. I think you all know it as well.

Today, as she smiles down on us, her legacy lives on.

If your heart hurts as you say goodbye, remember this. "If a small part of you is living the way she did, be grateful. Her spirit and her joy live on in you."

In the years following Kristen's passing her husband Mike remarried. Sales of the legacy book "Ornament" helped raise thousands of dollars for their three son's post-secondary education. Each year during the presentation of the Singing Christmas Tree at the Northern Alberta Jubilee Auditorium a single star is lighted, and Kristen's life is honoured. Her parents, sister Kennedy, and the John Cameron Changing Lives Foundation are dedicated to ensuring her faith, hope, and joy are never forgotten.

Kristen's prayers were not answered on earth the way any of us expected. We hold on to the same hope of heaven that held Kristen to her last moments on earth.

Music was her gift. Worship is her legacy.

To read Kristen's full story, purchase your copy of *Ornament: The Faith Hope and Joy of Kristen Fersovitch.* Hardcover copies are $10 plus shipping. To order your copy text BOOK to 780-707-5569 or email bob@revwords.com

CHAPTER NINE

Brenda Peake – Depression: The New Leprosy?

One of the finest lessons nature can teach us is that of hope.
She shows us hope realized with every bud that blossoms and
every bird that learns to fly.
~ Author unknown

I was first diagnosed with clinical depression in the early 1980s.

Not every person who is depressed experiences the same symptoms. Some people have many, others just a few. Severity varies with individuals and changes over time.

Sadness, anxiety, and apathy plagued me. I was terribly hopeless and pessimistic. I felt guilty because I was ill. I thought I had no control over my life or my decision-making ability. I didn't really care much about what the kids were doing or what was happening at home. I had limited energy and was tired all the time. Gaining 20 pounds made me have even lower self-esteem.

We had moved to Edmonton a few years earlier and were quite involved with foster parenting. We had two children of our own, one permanent ward who was severely handicapped who is now a permanent part of our family and 22 other foster children over four years. I was working part-time as a nurse in a job I really enjoyed. I felt very lonely in the church setting at that time as I thought we had not made any friends. We were involved in our children's activities but nothing for ourselves. My parents had moved to Africa, and I felt responsible for maintaining family unity here while they were away.

As a nurse, I knew what was happening to me, but I thoroughly rejected it. That was almost 40 years ago, I was about 25 years old. I was a Christian, and depression did not happen to Christians. I felt that if I trusted God and prayed, I should be better. Well, I wasn't. I could not allow myself to believe that it was a chemical imbalance within my body that was causing these symptoms.

Finally, I went to the doctor who prescribed medication, and I started seeing a counselor. I learned some new coping mechanisms, but mostly I talked…. and talked… and talked. Finally, after about a year, I was feeling better. Life was more normal. I didn't cry as much, and life at home was ok. I never told anyone what I had gone through. I didn't even talk to Rod about it much, because I was very embarrassed with this diagnosis.

To begin treatment, your physician must first diagnose you. You have to admit there is a problem—out loud to someone else. You will likely be started on medications. They often take 3-8 weeks before the full therapeutic effect occurs, so it is a long slow process to find the right drugs and the proper dosages. Once the individual is feeling better, it is crucial to continue on the medications until the doctor discontinues it to prevent a recurrence. Then they are usually stopped gradually. Antidepressants are not habit forming

Life went on. The kids grew up. We were busy at work and in the Church. I loved my job. We no longer had temporary foster children but had developed a permanent relationship with one of the foster children. Her name is Jennifer. She was diagnosed as deaf, blind, and retarded. She is also developmentally delayed.

In the early 90's we were transferred to Whitehorse. This was an exciting change, but still hard. Our oldest daughter Julie was starting University, so didn't move with us. Jocelyn came with us to finish her last two years of high school in the Yukon. Jenni stayed in Edmonton because there was no school for her up north. Rod had a challenging job. I had a job that was even better than anything I had in Edmonton. I was working in Labor and Delivery and Hospital Administration in Whitehorse. It was fun and exciting.

But life wasn't all that good. Julie had received some tainted blood during a surgical procedure as a young teenager. She was now getting chemotherapy for Hepatitis C. She was alone in Edmonton going through that.

I felt guilty.

Jenni was having lots of difficulty with violence and was in detention in Edmonton. I felt guilty about that.

Jocelyn had finished high school and was back in Edmonton. We had an empty nest the year I turned 40.

We had a series of unexpected infant deaths in the hospital—no one's fault—but it affected me very badly. There was a shortage of nurses there, and we had to work mandatory overtime—usually nine 12-hours shifts in two weeks as well as medivacs to Edmonton or Vancouver. I was exhausted and often working on adrenaline only.

Seasonal Affective Disorder (SAD)—which is depression caused by a shortage of sunlight, could also have been a factor. Whatever it was—the depression came back. I cried all the time. I managed OK at work, but at home it was awful. I became a hermit.

There were long periods that I would hardly talk to Rod. I would sleep very little and often went to work on three hours of sleep. Just before we were transferred back to Edmonton, I knew that I had to get back on track and I saw my family doctor who started treatment again. I had medication and counseling.

I was still a Christian. We sang in the choir. We went to Bible study, but I never felt I could share with anyone.

Depression is like leprosy. No one talks about it. It is ignored—especially in the church circles—and the people who are in depression feel even more isolated.

Often I would try to make comments about people with depression to sound out some of our friends, but the remarks I received in return were about people who "couldn't cope or should pray more, or maybe were nuts anyway," so it underscored my feeling that I was inadequate. I felt more alone and lost.

In the middle of it all, we moved back to Edmonton. We were thrilled. Julie was getting married in a few weeks. I found a job that was OK, certainly not exciting, but it helped pay the bills. We began attending back at Central Tabernacle and began establishing some old relationships. Life was good.

Well, not really.
I stopped my treatment—on my own. I cried even more. I slept even less. I had headaches all the time—often taking over 30 Tylenol a day.

I became suicidal.

I remember praying that I would not carry out any of my plans, but that was the only time I could or would pray. I shut out our friends—church and work. I didn't socialize. My feelings were hurt all the time. I was very sensitive. I knew everyone hated me. Rod and I had been attending a Bible study group, but I stopped going.

People recognized there was something wrong with me. I remember some people asking if I was OK. I would snap at them and turn away. A few people sent cards, but because I didn't respond, most contacts stopped.

I finally realized the hopelessness of trying to get better on my own, so I went back to the doctor and started on medication for a year. Since then, I have been well.

Is life perfect now? No. Jenni is still severely handicapped and presents us with many challenges every day. I am still busy at church, home, and socially. However, I am trying to look after myself better physically, spiritually, and emotionally. We go to the gym or do physical activity regularly. I allow myself to decline some of the opportunities I am given to do more things at church. I have even said no to my kids a time or two.

Now I feel cautious. It may happen again, but I know how to find appropriate help right away, and I recognize that I would need to do that. I know that God still loves me, and I am important to him. I will not make the mistake of shutting out and not forgiving other people. I will ask for help.

Because of my experiences, I have become more forgiving, more sensitive to others and their moods, and their need for inclusion. I am trying to be less judgmental. I know that if I cannot control my thoughts, I can go to God and he will help me. I will give myself permission to be the way I am.

A crucial thing is, don't give up on people with depression. They are not ignoring you or unfriendly. They are scared and hurting and feeling terribly alone. They want to have friends and be happy, but they don't feel they deserve it.

Bob asked me if the church was helpful and supportive to me during my depression. I don't think so—but I'm not sure because I was in a place that didn't allow me to accept help. Maybe it was there, and I didn't feel it. As a rule, people don't understand depression.

I shut people out in a cold hard way, and then no one tried again.

Be persistent. Love the unlovable—because a depressed person feels unlovable.

The only person I felt I could talk to was a lady who had also experienced severe depression after the death of her brother. She was quite open about it and made me feel accepted. That is one of the reasons I am telling you this today.

People who experience depression do not need to hide. They do not need to feel unloved or unchristian. God still loves them. We need to show love to them in as many ways as we can. We need to remember that we are not here on earth to see through one another, but to see one another through—through all of the things that could happen in life.

The most important thing to remember is that depression is manageable and recovery is highly likely if approached sensibly and skillfully. If you feel like you may be depressed, the best thing you can do for yourself is to recognize that you have to do something different if you want to escape its hold on you.

If you think you know someone who may be depressed, support them, encourage them to get help, be there for them. Don't give up. Make them feel accepted and acceptable. Don't demean them because of their fears or insecurity.

Listen to them.

Be their friend.

Pray with them.

Help them to remember that God still loves and cares for them. There are lots of treatments that can help you—but you have to make the first step. Be assured that the success rate in treatments very high.

The biggest obstacle to getting help is often the person's attitude. Many people think that depression will go away by itself, or they are too old to get help, or that getting help is a sign of weakness or moral failure. This is wrong.

People suffer mental and physical pain that causes them to suffer in silence. Why? Because of the stigma attached to depression.

The typical Christian waits 20 years to talk about the symptoms of depression. 12% said they would take medication for depression. 78% said they would wait for the symptoms to pass.

At one time, people who had seeing problems were stigmatized by wearing glasses. But then as people wore glasses and they could see it made a difference. Blurred vision is corrected by glasses. In the same way that blurred vision can be fixed, fuzzy thinking can be bettered.

Medication corrects chemical imbalances. Medication helps to put you on level ground to enable you to use spiritual strategy. Antidepressants are not mood altering drugs.

Depression is the only medical condition with spiritual symptoms. There are several different symptoms of depression.

They include:
- Persistent sad, anxious or empty mood
- Feelings of hopelessness or pessimism
- Feelings of guilt, worthlessness or helplessness
- Loss of interest or pleasure in hobbies and activities that once were enjoyed
- Decreased energy, fatigue
- Difficulty concentrating, remembering, making decisions
- Insomnia, early morning awakening, or oversleeping
- Appetite changes—weight loss or weight gain
- Thoughts of death or suicide, suicide attempts
- Restlessness or irritability
- Persistent physical symptoms that do not respond to treatment such as headaches, digestive disorders, and chronic pain

Depression is treatable, and I have proven it.

CHAPTER TEN

Phyllis Fisher – Love Never Lets Go

Your hopes, dreams and aspirations are legitimate. They are
trying to take you airborne, above the clouds, above the
storms, if you only let them.
~ William James

"Gone to get a kidney. Love, Phyllis"

That was so Phyllis.

The hurried note left on the table for her new husband Bruce was a matter-of-fact reminder of how Phyllis approached life.

Minutes earlier, she received a phone call from her attending physician. It was the call she had long anticipated and prayed for.

"You need to get to the hospital right away."

"I can't."

"What do you mean you can't?"

"I've got to take a bus because there is no one to drive me."

Her doctor pointedly told her, "No. Take a taxi."

"I don't have any money to pay for a taxi."

She could feel the urgency in her doctor's voice as he told her to call a taxi, and he would pay for it.

"Get here. Now."

On the way to the hospital, Phyllis could hardly contain her joy. She eagerly informed the taxi driver, "I'm going to get a kidney." No response. As though he didn't just hear the best news in the entire universe.

What can you do when you have no one to share your excitement with? She thought she'd explode but better not because her dream was so close to coming true.

"Bruce will be so happy."

When she arrived at the hospital, attendants were impatiently waiting for her. As she got out of the taxi, they scolded, "Where have you been?"

Phyllis explained, "Well, I had to pack my suitcase."

As she lay on the gurney waiting for the donor's kidney, Phyllis was sobered by the thought that someone else died for her to be the recipient of this kidney.
"I'm no one special, Lord. Why me?"

Never in her wildest dreams would she have envisioned the unique purpose that God had for that donated organ. Even further from her imagination was the fact she would have not one, but two kidney transplants in her lifetime, and become one of the longest surviving transplant patients in Canadian history.

How could she have known this kidney would change the future for her and literally thousands of people who would be influenced by Phyllis Ryan Fisher.

The effects of Phyllis' life are forever rippling out in ever-expanding circles of love. If you haven't yet felt their influence, you soon will.

Phyllis Ryan Fisher was born in Toronto just before the Christmas of '47 to a loving and resourceful mother who in post-war years either cared directly for Phyllis or made sure she was nurtured in wonderful homes surrounded by people who "adopted" her into their families.

Although Phyllis was an only child, she collected moms and dads and sisters along the way that enriched her life and helped mold her into the lady she grew to be. This small-town girl loved the water and the Kawartha Lakes country where she grew up –

especially her beloved "Coby" - and never forgot the friends who all loved her as a local girl who was going to make her mark in life.

Much of her life was tinged by the effects of rejection and abandonment. Phyllis learned that rejection isn't just an emotion we feel. It's a message that's sent to the core of who we are, causing us to believe lies about ourselves, others, and God. We connect our experiences today to something harsh someone once said.

That person's line becomes a label.

The label becomes a lie.

And the lie becomes a liability in how we think about ourselves and interact in every future relationship.

At the tender age of eight, Phyllis had a real experience with the love of God. Alone in her room, reading her Bible, her heart heard God say that He would not reject her. She was embraced by a love that would never let go. Her entire life became salt and light to people far from God.

During three wonderful years at Eastern Pentecostal Bible College, she made friends that cared about and reached out to Phyllis for the rest of her life. The tributes via social media after her passing are a testament to the way she could welcome people into her life and love them like family.

Phyllis was struck with a severe illness soon after college and met the challenge of committing her vows to Bruce Fisher by asking to be released from the hospital the night before her wedding and then returning to a rigorous schedule of kidney dialysis after a couple of days honeymooning in Niagara Falls in October of 1968.

Phyllis eventually received a kidney from an unknown donor, whose family in their grief from losing a daughter in a fatal Toronto car accident, contributed the gift of life to a critically ill, unidentified recipient. They probably do not know that their gift kept Phyllis alive and in excellent renal health for over thirty years – one of Canada's longest living transplant recipients. Telling her story was a way for Phyllis to encourage more organ donations and inspire those needing a transplant to hold on to hope.

From these challenging days just to stay alive, Phyllis was to begin a journey that defied the best predictions of her dedicated doctors. They suggested that she would never be far away from the health support of the medical community in Toronto, never be a mother, probably not live for many years as transplantation was a relatively new development in medical science. And yes, she could not take on the responsibilities of a career.

In hindsight, her family details that Phyllis was not only able to be released from her caring medical community in Toronto, but she also ended up moving to Kingston, Ontario, Lyttleton, Saint John, and Moncton, all in New Brunswick, Montreal, Quebec and then to Edmonton, Alberta.

She shared her love with wonderful congregations of these towns and cities and gained innumerable friends along the way. During these years she accepted and functioned at a high level as a pastor's wife, encourager-in-chief to many young people, led bible studies, taught Sunday School, counselled those whose trust she accepted and cherished. During her time in Moncton, two French-speaking churches were planted on the Gaspe coast as a result of evangelistic Bible studies she led with the assistance of a French-speaking Mrs. Bailey.

Phyllis became a preacher in her own right and was recognized by her denomination by being ordained. Phyllis also moved to and lived in Sylvan Lake and Ponoka during her tenure as a chaplain.

In 1972 Phyllis became a mother to her son Shawn. Her gifts as a mom were evident immediately, and she couldn't wait to receive her daughter, Robyn in 1975. Phyllis took hold of her home and welded four unrelated-by-blood members into the loving family that she presided over to her death.

With equal enthusiasm, she embraced the arrival of grandsons Kaiden and Ryland, then later, Hailey and Hannah. Who could have ever imagined that this family would come into being and be glued together by the love and encouragement of this extraordinary lady besought by illness most of her life?

When Bruce was sidelined by illness for many years, Phyllis just got on with life and fashioned a career in Chaplaincy that saw her associate with wonderful supervisors and fellow students and then goes on to become a practical guide and encourager to so many in health institutions and prison facilities.

While balancing home and career and addressing medical challenges, Phyllis pursued and obtained a Masters Degree in her field.

It was also during this time that another fellow professional, Karen McLeod, extended to Phyllis the gift of life by becoming a living donor and giving one of her own kidneys after Phyllis' original kidney failed. The Fishers are forever grateful to Karen.

Later in life, Phyllis faced a diagnosis of cancer with the same composure and hope that saw her through the worst of life's challenges. Faith, selflessness, and courage saw her through surgeries, radiation treatments, and hospital stays. But the cancer was tenacious, and her pain was debilitating. She weakened to the point of preparing for death.

When she asked me to write a memoir for her grandchildren, my "Yes" was out of my mouth before I fully understood the sacred commitment I was making. But how could I - or anyone - say "no" to Phyllis? Bruce and Phyllis were pastors to Jocelyn in Saint John and later myself at Central Tabernacle. In a rare and treasured turnaround, we became their pastors at North Pointe.

The significance of this rare relationship was never lost on us. Phyllis was Jocelyn's biggest cheerleader. "She made me feel like I could be the senior pastor's wife of a significant kingdom church."

Creating a legacy piece for her grandchildren was a privilege. Often her granddaughters would arrive as I was leaving from our interviews.

Though she was born into a family that didn't work, she knew how to make her family work.

Phyllis never used her illness or pain to deflect her drive to care for people, and it was easy for those looking on to think she never had a care in the world beyond those they knew about.

Phyllis wanted people to know that transplants work. She conferred with many patients who were afraid to have a transplant, and when she told them how long she had her transplant, they'd respond, "You have been how long?!" When she got to thirty years as a transplant patient, she made the story and celebration about encouraging other people, not about her.

Our writing journey began in her living room on March 9, 2017. We met for a second interview on March 17th - Saint Patrick's Day. A fitting time as Phyllis was proud of her Irish heritage. There was no blarney in her answer when I asked how she was feeling. "I'm at a five out of ten on a pain scale. Three would be a threshold where some attention needs to be paid to my pain level. But that's OK."

On March 23rd, I was introduced to a friend of Phyllis' as well as the woman who donated one of her kidneys to Phyllis in 2006. I listened in on a lively conversation. None of us had any idea that two months later to the day Phyllis would be in heaven.

Phyllis and I met again on March 31st, April 5th, and April 18th. Ministry commitments took me out of town for the next three weeks. I fully expected to see her in the 2nd week of May. But by then, she was in tertiary care.

Though tending to prefer background roles in ministry, Phyllis could be quite bold when she felt the prompting of the Holy Spirit. She was known for giving public expressions during church services – a word of encouragement or exhortation. She shared what she felt were words from the Lord, and she often received affirmations, "That was just what I needed to hear."

Phyllis was effervescent, genuinely loved, and accepted people as they were. She didn't have a judgmental bone in her body. Making other people feel recognized and essential was Phyllis' mission.

She will always be remembered for her zest for life and the incredible contributions she made to so many people.

A copy of "Phyllis: Love Never Lets Go" is available for $10 plus shipping by texting LOVE to 780-707-5569 or emailing bob@revwords.com

CHAPTER ELEVEN

Jocelyn Jones – Wicked Strong

You are stronger than you think.

Jocelyn's voice sounded a million miles away.

Unreal.

Words I never expected to hear from my wife.

Too many people I love had whispered those same words. They'd been uttered with tears and a tone that sounded scared and sacred. My mom said the same words when my mind couldn't grasp the significance.

Monday, March 12, 2018. I was just about to officiate a funeral service. One of North Pointe's support staff summoned me from the platform. "Jocelyn needs you." My silent expression warned, "Can't you see I'm about to start the service?"

Her response, "Now" was all it took to sound an alarm.

Jocelyn was sitting on the edge of a chair in my office. The Kleenex she held was failing to soak up her tears. Her body language spoke volumes. Whatever had happened, I knew our world just changed forever. An accident? Her parents? Our sons? Not a grandchild?

"My doctor called. He says I have endometrial cancer."

Cancer.

Not cancer.

How could this be happening to Jocelyn?

What followed was a blur of doctor's appointments, oncologist consults, scheduling surgery, pre-op briefings, calling family, and sharing with friends who are cancer survivors. The words "so sorry" were heard from so many.

We prayed back fear.

Her continual encouragement was, "Go and do what you need to do. I'll be OK." Two days later we embarked on a rigorous process of a Discovery Week for the church family we pastored. There were effectiveness coaches to meet with, probing interview questions, Board meetings, and evaluations. Jocelyn didn't want her diagnosis to delay or be a distraction from our work to help revitalize North Pointe. We journeyed alone in the discovery process of our own.

One solace Jocelyn held on to came from our Caribbean cruise two months earlier. In the quiet enjoyment of sun and silence on the 14th deck of the Navigator of the Seas, she heard the words, "You're going to be OK." They were inaudible but unforgettable.

Her first reactions were "The ship's going to sink" and "Bob's going to die." On March 12th, the realization came; those words were meant for her. "You're going to be OK."

"OK" is a good thing. Jocelyn had cancer, but she was going to be OK. How that would come to be was not relevant. She would be OK.

The words were a gift to strengthen Jocelyn before she needed the strength.

A dear friend and cancer survivor brought home a bracelet from her trip to Boston. The inscription on the bracelet was "Wicked Strong." The phrase became Jocelyn's go-to words. Unusual wording for a pastor's wife - but that's Jocelyn.

The initial surgery date of April 17th was postponed until April 26th because Jocelyn was in ill health. Each day of delay felt like a week.

On the morning of surgery, the alarm clock sounded at 4:20am. Not that we needed its help to wake up. Sleep was hard to come by. Going out our front door at 5:12am, a bird was singing. As we drove out of St Albert along Mark Messier Way, we happened across a rabbit – Jocelyn's favorite animal. All good.

We checked in at the Lois Hole Hospital For Women and sat in a waiting area. A dedication plaque on the wall acknowledged the contributions of "The Wiebe Family" – friends of ours.

Connie was Jocelyn's prep nurse. She was genial, calming, light-hearted and humorous – suggesting I go to nearby Kingsway Mall to buy gifts for my wife. She complimented Jocelyn on the purple coloring in her hair. Seems like everybody loved the purple, including a Dr. Mills who expressed surprise at seeing the choice of color. It makes a woman feel good.

On the day of the surgery, a nurse from North Pointe "happened" to be scheduled to work in the surgery-prep ward. Ruth's familiarity was a godsend. Leading up to surgery, Jocelyn encountered four people from North Pointe at four different medical appointments. Godwinks – that's what we call experiences which make you ask, "What are the odds of that?" They were reassurances that God had his eye on Jocelyn. After all, she was going to be OK, right?

Jocelyn's brother - a paramedic - showed up on the ward in his work clothes. We prayed together before surgery.

"Time to go." The moment came all too quickly. We kissed. Jocelyn was wheeled out of her room and onto the elevator. As the doors closed, Jocelyn gave me two thumbs up, smiled, and declared, "Wicked strong!"

Tears still come to my eyes as I write this. My wife of thirty-nine years was in the good hands of God and those of her surgeon.

Observations From My Journey

Being diagnosed with cancer was the last thing I expected. Bob and I were entirely preoccupied with our pastoral ministry at North Pointe. I loved the women who were a part of our Bible studies and community events. We were about to begin a long journey of discovery in our church and work to vitalize our mission and purpose. I didn't have time to have cancer.

So my oncologist's call was shocking, to say the least. I was on my heels.

But then we did what we've always done over our four decades of ministry – we trusted God, put His work first, told our families, solicited prayer, and got back down to business.

Was I scared?

Yes.

But I did have a deep assurance that I would be OK. I carried that deposit of hope in my spirit for two months. And that hope carried me through.

Are you facing cancer? God is faithful. Even when you feel faithless.

Lean into Him. Prayer doesn't have to be eloquent or phrased correctly to be effective. "Help me Jesus" is a good prayer. He's as close as the mention of his name.

I learned that I don't have to plead with God for help but to simply claim what Jesus has already provided for me.

And I learned so much more.

A cancer diagnosis compels you to think about what and who is important.

Brenda, my friend, who is a nurse, came back to Edmonton from Phoenix just to be with me. She drove straight to the hospital before I went into surgery. Brenda stayed in our home for three days to nurse me back to strength. Our neighbors and friends came in to visit, talk, drink coffee, share meals, walk together, iron shirts, wash dishes, and more.

It's OK for people of faith to feel scared with a cancer diagnosis.

Cancer is cancer. There is no minor cancer when it's your cancer. Never say to a cancer patient, "That's good. It's not terminal like..."

Conversations about cancer are hard. Talking about a diagnosis makes it "real." Emotions run high in patients and family members. Cancer is all they think about but don't want to talk about.

Cancer patients struggle against going to the dark places and answering the "What if" questions with the worst.

People with cancer have to battle hard to prevent fear from tipping the scales against faith.

Don't rush your recovery. Three steps forward. Rest. One more step. Rest. Rinse. Repeat. Lean into the support that others offer.

Every physician, surgeon, and nurse who served us did so with stellar professionalism, compassion, and empathy. We are blessed in Alberta with skilled and dedicated health care providers.

The prayers, phone calls, texts, emails, messages, meals, cards, bouquets, baking, and home visits from friends and family carried us.

When I was diagnosed with cancer, I wanted to talk about my cancer with people who had faced cancer. After my surgery and recovery, I wanted to hear from people who let me know I would be OK. After my doctors told me I was "cancer free," I didn't want to talk about cancer.

Cancer survivors rule.

Are you or a loved one facing cancer? What is your journey?

We started a ministry called "Supporting the Fighters." You can't – and shouldn't – fight cancer alone. We need each other. Many people will be helpful if you let them know your needs. We developed a trusted network of empathetic people who will lean in when others walk away.

Follow us on Facebook at Supporting the Fighters.

BOB JONES

CHAPTER TWELVE

Bob and Jocelyn – Hope Dispensers

People who build hope into their own lives and who share
hope with others become powerful people.
~ Zig Ziglar

We wish someone had told us we were going to OK.

Long before the lawsuit, the hate mail, the identity theft, the petition to end our leadership, the letter writing campaign, the threatening phone calls, and adversarial congregational meetings.

Long before the setbacks, adversity, rejection, disappointments, discouragement, and despair.

Long before we had come to believe we were terrible people and worse pastors.
Don't let anyone tell you that living a life of faith is a crutch for the weak.

Only the courageous survive.

Living by faith means you may get delivered from the mouth of lions, or you may end up eaten alive by said lions. Or well-intentioned dragons.

Leading change requires faith. And courage. Relocating a historic, urban, regionalized church, with an iconic facility built on sacred ground to a farmer's field on the frontier of a major Canadian city is a wee bit of a change.

We embarked in May 2000 on our relocation journey with real confidence. Not too long into the process, it dawned on us that confidence is what you have before you fully understand the situation. Change is resisted because the world is full of people whose notion of a satisfactory future is a return to an idealized past.

Nineteen Mays later life is different.

We made it our responsibility to see to it that North Pointe thrives as a community of people in process; where the curious, the unconvinced, the skeptical, and the used-to-believe, as well as the committed, informed and sold-out, come as they are together around the conviction that Jesus is the Savior, the Son of the living God.

North Pointe is a vitalized, come as you are, life-giving, mission-driven church, devoted to Jesus, and His love for the world. People are discovering real hope, new life, and lasting purpose.

For every setback, we discovered a greater comeback on the other side of hope.

We learned to never, ever, ever, ever quit. The easiest thing to do it quit. There is a significant difference between finishing and quitting. The difference is hope. To quit is to give up hope. To finish is to find a new purpose with hope.

Hope says, "You'll get through this."

In no way are those words a trite offering to desperate people at the end of their rope.

"You'll get through this" is a substantive word of hope.

Hope is not wishful thinking but a confident expectation of future good.

The confident expectation is birthed through perspective – of seeing your circumstances through God's eyes.

Where you see a perfect mess, God sees a perfect chance to send you a message about Himself.

The God of the Bible is not passive. God entered our sufferings.

The Christian theology of suffering is built around the fact that God loves us so profoundly that He became like us. He was "perfected" by His sufferings. Hebrews 2:10 (NIV). Jesus suffered death so that he "might taste death for everyone." Hebrews 2:9 (NIV)

Jesus suffered when he was tempted so that he can help those who are being tempted. Hebrews 2:19, (NIV) "My Father, if it is possible, may this cup be taken from me. Yet not as I will, but as you will." Matthew 26:39 (NIV)

Jesus shows that suffering is ultimately about the answer to the question of God, "Am I enough for you? Is my goodness trustworthy?"

Those are the two sources of suffering: things that we've brought on ourselves, and things are done to us. God's message through Scripture is that he gets us through both types.

There are many stories in the Bible of the means God uses for deliverance. The story of Joseph is a prime example.

Joseph was a young man sold into slavery by his jealous brothers. He worked for an Egyptian master and ended up in prison on the short end of a false accusation. The reason Joseph survived in jail in Egypt was that God was with him. In the Joseph story, after he's sold into slavery, five times in that narrative we read, "God was with him."

The narrator wants to make the point that Joseph is doing well, not because Joseph is good, but because God is good.

Secondly, but equally important is Joseph's theology of suffering.

His beliefs about God made sense of how he had gotten through the evil episodes in his life.

Many people don't realize that there's even a possibility God is sovereign and He can use suffering for good.

Joseph's theology of suffering is revealed in Genesis 50:20 when he said to his brothers,

"You intended it for evil, but God intended it for good." It's a concise, powerful statement that says, "Yes, there's evil in the world. But there's still a God, even though there's evil, and God can take that evil and turn it into something good."

God can turn evil intentions into good outcomes.

Are you facing cancer, sexual abuse, mental illness, or loss? For many women, those are a prison, if not death sentences. But they don't have to be. The women in this book show there is hope to get through the most heartrending trauma.

Hope is not turning a blind eye to reality or wishful thinking.

Hope is not pretending problems don't exist.

Hope is the belief problems won't last forever.

Hurts will be healed.

Difficulties will be overcome.

When you challenge your outlook, you change your life.

We live in a beautiful, tragic, complicated world. Emotional, intellectual, and spiritual turbulence is a part of life. Confusion creates uncertainty.

Over coffee, I've listened to many believers say, "I struggle with my faith. It's funny because I believe very powerfully in God and all that He can do and yet I have so many doubts."

Does God hear my prayers?
Is the Bible really true?
Will God lead me and keep me safe?
With so much suffering, how can you believe God to be good?
Is God really in control?

Stephanie Williams grew up in Indiana. Hers was a typical mid-west American upbringing. Every Sunday her family took Steph to church and Sunday School. From a young age, she knew God was calling her to be a missionary. Fast forward to when she met Charles Wesco, a young man who equally felt called to be a missionary. They married, had eight kids all while Charles served as a pastor. In 2015 the Wescos felt God was directing them to become missionaries to Cameroon, a nation tearing apart from civil war. The following three years were spent training and raising money. Charles and Stephanie went all in by selling everything they owned, including their home.

The Wescos taught and lived by the saying, "Life begins at the end of your comfort zone." After tearful farewells to family and friends, they left their comfort zone and followed their dream. On October 18th, 2018 all ten Wescos arrived in Cameroon and started to settle into their new life.

Twelve days later, Stephanie and Charles were traveling in a vehicle with an experienced missionary. They were out shopping in a "safe" zone, supposedly far away from rebel violence. Their conversation suddenly died as bullets penetrated the windshield, striking Charles twice. He was gone in an instant.

Charles Wesco prepared his whole life to serve God. He dedicated his marriage, parenting, and career to serving God. He spent three years raising money to go to Cameroon, the place God was calling him to. He was in place for 12 days. Stephanie, now a widow with eight children ages 2-13 grieved, "I want to wake up from this horrific nightmare."

What do you do when your dream becomes a nightmare?

"When John, who was in prison, heard about the deeds of the Messiah, he sent his disciples ³ to ask him, "Are you the one who is to come, or should we expect someone else?" ⁴ Jesus replied, "Go back and report to John what you hear and see: ⁵ The blind receive sight, the lame walk, those who have leprosy are cleansed, the deaf hear, the dead are raised, and the good news is proclaimed to the poor. ⁶ Blessed is anyone who does not stumble on account of me." Matthew 11:2-6 (NIV)

John the Baptist was a cousin to Jesus - the first prophet in Israel in over 400 years. John spent his whole life preparing. He lived in the desert, wore a cloak made of camel's hair and subsisted on a diet of locusts. He was popular with a considerable following.

John knew he was chosen by God to be the messenger of the Messiah. He was confident of his mission and lived on purpose. Set apart. Obedient. Powerful. He baptized those who responded to his preaching in the Jordan River. Jesus called him "the greatest man who ever lived."

John saw the Spirit of God like a dove descend on Jesus. He heard a voice from heaven. "This is my beloved Son."

What is clear is that when the revelation came, it was an overwhelming experience for John. He saw the Messiah. He began to promote Jesus as the Messiah. When his followers followed Jesus, he celebrated their choice. "He must increase. I must decrease." John not only decreased, but he also disappeared.

John languished in a filthy prison for over 18 months. He had expected this. Prophets who rebuke sinful kings usually do not fare well. What he hadn't expected was to be tormented by such oppressive doubts and fears. John had never doubted that Jesus was the Christ. But stuck alone in this cell he was assaulted by horrible, accusing thoughts.

"Why wasn't something important happening? When is Jesus going to start the kingdom? When will our oppressors be judged? When will I be released? Is Jesus really the Messiah? What if I was wrong?"

John had expectations. Messiah would overthrow the Roman oppressors, and establish a kingdom of freedom, peace, righteousness. None of this was happening.

He tried to recall all the prophecies and signs that had seemed so clear to him before. But it was difficult to think straight. Comfort just wouldn't stick to his soul. Doubts buzzed around his brain like the flies around his face. The events he witnessed that had been so compelling had lost their effect.

Can you relate? Have you been through a time when you felt overwhelmed? Your questions of God had no answers? Circumstances were not working out. Dreams became a nightmare.

The disconnect between how John thought things should work and how life actually turned out produced a crisis of faith and hope.

John's fundamental error was being mistaken about the Messiah's work and the future. Jesus was not what John expected. But Jesus is what God intended. Faith in God doesn't follow a script—even if that script is the Bible.

What if God is not acting as you expect Him to? What if your questions or doubts are not evidence of a lack of faith but are evidence of God's prompting in your life? Challenging your outlook.

So John sent two of his closest disciples to ask Jesus, "Are you the one who is to come, or shall we look for another?"

Jesus invited John's friends to sit near him as he healed the sick and delivered many from demonic prisons.

"Tell John what you have heard and seen: the blind receive their sight, the lame walk, lepers are cleansed, and the deaf hear, the dead are raised up, and the poor have the gospel preached to them."

John would recognize those words. Jesus used words from a prophecy from Isaiah - a familiar prophecy about the Messiah. Jesus is saying, "I am the Messiah." Jesus uses Old Testament verses to comfort John. This promise would bring the peace John needed to sustain him for the few problematic days he had remaining.

Jesus leaves out one part of the Scripture – about setting the captives free. It's a message to John. He would remain in prison. But not saying this he told John everything he needed to know.

And tell him, 'God blesses those who do not turn away because of me.'" (NLT)

The one thing people of faith have in common is doubt.

The longer I've lived, and the more I've sought to know and understand God, the more I'm confident that doubts are essential to spiritual maturity.

The hurtful response to doubting and questioning is to keep people in a bubble - or simply to dismiss their questions and advise them to "pray harder," "read the Bible," or "just believe."

The healthy response is to learn how to challenge your outlook.

111

1. Learn to doubt your doubts. Be honest with the fact you have doubts. Believers who don't have doubts are dangerous. People who don't know how to question can be encouraged to develop critical thinking. Be merciful to the doubtful.

2. Doubting isn't smarter than believing. Why would we doubt our faith or beliefs or convictions, but we don't doubt our doubts?

3. Ask honest questions. Questioning your beliefs is the best defense against questioning God. Distinguish between your ideas about God from who God is.

4. Faith is not 100% certainty. Faith is not finite answers to infinite questions. If you were completely certain of everything, you wouldn't need faith. Without faith, it's impossible to please God.

5. The opposite of faith is not doubt; it's when you have it all figured out.

Faith is not fantasy. Faith is founded in fact. Jesus of Nazareth rose from the dead is grounded in reliable accounts from eyewitnesses and persons informed by those who saw a formerly dead man alive.

The documentary evidence is sound, and those bearing witness to what they saw made clear they meant what they said. Peter, one of the eyewitnesses, explained years later, "We did not follow cleverly devised myths when we made known to you the power and coming of our Lord Jesus Christ, but we were eyewitnesses" (2 Pet. 1:16).

The insistence of Jesus's early followers that what they asserted was true implies they knew it sounded incredible. That's why they went to such lengths to provide careful accounts of what they'd seen and heard. The Gospel accounts have no ring of fantasy about them.

6. Doubt confronted will make faith stronger. The struggle you're in today is building the faith you'll need for tomorrow.

7. Let your doubts lead you to worship.

Intellectual and spiritual growth will lead you, not to overconfidence in your ability to figure God out but to your knees in worshiping a good God who is beyond figuring out.

And as in Stephanie Wesco's case, forgiveness.
"His life focus was seeking to cause others to love Jesus and serve him. My prayer is that somehow, someway Jesus will be glorified through Charles' death and that God will not let his death have been in vain."

In April 2019 doctors discovered tumors in Stephanie's liver. Her eight children were threatened with losing both parents to tragic circumstances. The tumors were found to be benign, but even before the diagnosis, Stephanie was steadfast in her hope that God will see them through this.

10 Observations About Getting Through Whatever You Face:

1. Be careful of short-term thinking - your struggles will not last forever, but you will. You still have your destiny.

2. You will never go where God is not. He is near whether you are happy or not.

3. God uses everything for His glory and our ultimate approval.

4. Don't make matters worse by doing something you'll later

regret.

5. Instead of trying to please others, focus on doing what pleases God.

6. See troubles as something God uses to develop your character and maturity for His glory.

7. While you wait, God works on your behalf. Waiting is sustained effort focused on God through prayer and belief.

8. You can either choose to trust God or turn away from Him.

9. While proud people are seldom grateful, grateful people see every day as a gift from God.

10. Trust God to take care of you.

You'll get through "this." Whatever your "this" is.

It won't be painless.

It won't be quick.

God will use your mess for good.

Don't be foolish or naive.

Don't despair.

You'll get through this.

Hope has substance. Hope is a person.

My hope is built on nothing less
Than Jesus blood and righteous
I dare not trust the sweetest frame

But wholly lean on Jesus' name.

Jesus is the source of eternal hope. Deciding to become a follower Jesus is the first step to a hope-filled future. How can you take that step? Pray to receive Jesus as your Savior, Healer, and God.

"Jesus, I surrender my past, future, and present to you. I've been living my own way, doing my own thing. I want to live your way. Send your Holy Spirit into my life to fill me, guide, and give me strength. Let me feel your work in my life. Thank you for hearing me and answering my prayer."

Let someone else know your decision.

Use the stories of hope in this book to find hope for the story you find yourself in. Share the book with others. Build hope into your life and become powerful by sharing your hope with others.

Act with hope. Send a thank you email to the people in each chapter. Purchase their book. Support their causes. Find them on Facebook and follow them. When they are in your area, go and hear them and make a point to meet them.

And by all means, hold on to hope.

Now the God of hope fill you with all joy and peace in believing, that you may abound in hope. ~ The Bible, Romans 15:13

Words matter. Keep your hope tank filled with ongoing stories of hope. We dispense them every week. Subscribe to REVwords at REVwords.com.

BOB JONES

EPILOGUE - HOPE QUOTES

Poets, preachers, politicians, presidents, philosophers, captains of industry, and all those who conquer their fears point to hope as a source of strength.

Hope does not put us to shame because God's love has been poured out into our hearts through the Holy Spirit. ~ Paul (Romans 5:5)

Expect to have hope rekindled. Expect your prayers to be answered in wondrous ways. The dry seasons in life do not last. The spring rains will come again. ~ Sarah Ban Breathnach

Faith goes up the stairs that love has built and looks out the window which hope has opened. ~ Charles Spurgeon

Where some see despair, others see hope. Hope then, like beauty, is in the eye of the beholder. ~ Wendy Edey

Forgiving means to pardon the unpardonable, Faith means believing the unbelievable and hoping means to hope when things are hopeless. ~ G. K. Chesterton

Why my soul, are you downcast? Put your hope in God, for I will yet praise him. ~ David (Psalm 42:5)

All the great spiritual leaders in history were people of hope. Abraham, Moses, Ruth, Mary, Jesus, all lived with a promise in their hearts that guided them toward the future without the need to know exactly what it would look like. Let's live with hope. ~ Henri Nouwen

But keep on working and hoping still.
For in spite of the grumblers who stand about,
somehow, it seems, all things work out.
~ Edgar Guest

This I call to mind and therefore I have hope. Because of the Lord's great love, we are not consumed, for his compassions never fail. They are new every morning; great is your faithfulness. ~ Jeremiah (Lamentations 3:21)

As for me, I watch in hope for the Lord, I wait for God my Saviour; my God will hear me. ~ Micah (Micah 7:7)

Hope is not the conviction that something will turn out well but the certainty that something makes sense, regardless of how it turns out. ~ Vaclav Havel

Hope is not a granted wish or a favor performed; no it is far greater than that. It is a zany, unpredictable dependence on a God who loves to surprise us out of our socks. ~ Max Lucado

Prepare a guest room for me for because I hope to be restored to you in answer to your prayers. ~ Paul (Philemon 1:22)

Change has a considerable psychological impact on the human mind. To the fearful, it is threatening because it means that things may get worse. To the hopeful, it is encouraging because things may get better. ~ King Whitney Jr

Consult not your fears but your hopes and dreams, think not about your frustrations, but about your unfulfilled potential. Concern yourself not with what you tried and failed in, but with what is still possible for you to do. ~ Pope John XXIII

Those who hope in the Lord will renew their strength. They will soar on wings like eagles; they will run and not grow weary, they will walk and not be faint. ~ Isaiah (Isaiah 40:31)

Every area of trouble gives out a ray of hope, and the one unchangeable certainty is that nothing is certain or unchangeable. ~ John Fitzgerald Kennedy

Every parent is at some time the father of the unreturned prodigal, with nothing to do but keep his house open to hope. ~ John Ciardi

Set your hope on the grace to be brought to you when Jesus Christ is revealed at his coming. ~ Peter (1 Peter 1:13)

Fear less, hope more; eat less, chew more; whine less, breathe more; talk less, say more; hate less, love more; and all good things are yours. ~ Swedish proverb

Have hope. Though clouds environs now, And gladness hides her face in scorn, Put thou the shadow from thy brow - No night but hath its morn. ~ J. C. F. von Schiller

Hope cherishes no illusions, nor does it yield to cynicism. ~ Father James Keller

Hope doesn't come from calculating whether the good news is winning out over the bad. It's simply a choice to take action. ~ Anna Lappe

Hope is a light we keep inside that no one can touch. ~ Jermaine J. Evans

Hope is a renewable option: If you run out of it at the end of the day, you get to start over in the morning. ~ Barbara Kingsolver

Hope is a risk that must be run. ~ Georges Bernanos

Hope is a state of mind, not of the world. Hope, in this deep and powerful sense, is not the same as joy that things are going well, or willingness to invest in enterprises that are obviously heading for success, but rather an ability to work for something because it is good. ~ Vaclav Havel

Hope is always available to us. When we feel defeated, we need only take a deep breath and say, Yes, and hope will reappear. ~ Monroe Forester

Hope is an adventure, a going forward, a confident search for a rewarding life. ~ Dr. Karl Menninger

Hope is both the earliest and the most indispensable virtue inherent in the state of being alive. If life is to be sustained, hope must remain, even where confidence is wounded, trust impaired. ~ Erik H. Erikson

Hope is brightest when it dawns from fears. ~ Sir Walter Scott

Hope is necessary in every condition. The miseries of poverty, sickness, of captivity, would, without this comfort, be insupportable. ~ Samuel Johnson

Hope is patience with the lamp lit. ~ Tertullian

Hope is the belief, more or less strong, that joy will come. ~ Sydney Smith

Hope is the feeling that life and work have a meaning. You either have it, or you don't, regardless of the state of the world that surrounds you. ~ Vaclav Havel

Hope is the feeling you have that the feeling you have isn't permanent. ~ Jean Kerr

Hope is the power of being cheerful in circumstances which we know to be desperate. ~ G. K. Chesterton

Hope is the word which God has written on the brow of every man. ~ Victor Hugo

Hope means believing in spite of the evidence and then watching the evidence change. ~ Jim Wallis

Hope opens doors where despair closes them. ~ Father James Keller

Hope unbelieved is always considered nonsense. But hope believed is history in the process of being changed. ~ Jim Wallis

I am not an optimist because I am not sure that everything ends well. Nor am I a pessimist, because I am not sure that everything ends badly. I just carry hope in my heart. ~ Vaclav Havel

I believe that imagination is stronger than knowledge. That myth is more potent than history. That dreams are more powerful than facts. That hope always triumphs over experience. That laughter is the only cure for grief. And I believe that love is stronger than death. ~ Robert Fulghum

I cannot imagine that I could strive for something if I did not carry hope in me. ~ Vaclav Havel

I know the world is filled with troubles and many injustices. But reality is as beautiful as it is ugly. I think it is just as important to sing about beautiful mornings as it is to talk about slums. I just couldn't write anything without hope in it. ~ Oscar Hammerstein

If it were not for hopes, the heart would break. ~ Thomas Fuller

If you lose hope, somehow you lose the vitality that keeps life moving, you lose that courage to be, that quality that helps you go on in spite of it all. And so today I still have a dream. ~ Martin Luther King, Jr.

If you wish to succeed in life, make perseverance your bosom friend, experience your wise counselor, caution your elder brother, and hope your guardian genius. ~ Joseph Addison

In the face of uncertainty, there is nothing wrong with hope. ~ Bernie S. Siegel

Isn't it the moment of most profound doubt that gives birth to new certainties? Perhaps hopelessness is the very soil that nourishes human hope; perhaps one could never find sense in life without first experiencing its absurdity. ~ Vaclav Havel

It has never been, and never will be, easy work! But the road that is built in hope is more pleasant to the traveler than the road built in despair, even though they both lead to the same destination. ~ Marion Zimmer Bradley

It is a fact of life that we find ourselves in unpleasant demoralizing situations which we can neither escape nor control. We can keep our morale and spirits high by using both coping and hoping humor. Coping humor laughs at the hopelessness in our situation. It gives us the courage to hang in there, but it does not bring hope. The uniqueness of hoping humor lies in its acceptance of life with all its dichotomies, contradictions, and incongruities. It celebrates the hope in human life. From one comes courage, from the other comes inspiration. ~ Cy Eberhart

It is history that teaches us to hope. ~ Robert E. Lee

Man is a creature of hope and invention, both of which belie the idea that things cannot be changed. ~ Tom Clancy

Men and women are limited not by the place of their birth, not by the color of their skin, but by the size of their hope. ~ John Johnson

Most of the important things in the world have been accomplished by people who have kept on trying when there seemed to be no hope at all. ~ Dale Carnegie

My great hope is to laugh as much as I cry; to get my work done and try to love somebody and have the courage to accept the love in return. ~ Maya Angelou

Never deprive someone of hope; it might be all they have. ~ H Jackson Brown Jr

Never talk defeat. Use words like hope, belief, faith, victory. ~ Norman Vincent Peale

Nothing worth doing is completed in our lifetime; therefore, we must be saved by hope. Nothing true or beautiful makes complete sense in any immediate context of history; therefore, we must be saved by faith. Nothing we do, however virtuous, can be accomplished alone; therefore, we are saved by love. ~ Reinhold Niebuhr

Of all the forces that make for a better world, none is so indispensable, none so powerful, as hope. Without hope, people are only half alive. With hope, they dream and think and work. ~ Charles Sawyer

One of the best safeguards of our hopes, I have suggested, is to be able to mark off the areas of hopelessness and to acknowledge them, to face them directly, not with despair but with the creative intent of keeping them from polluting all the areas of possibility. ~ William F. Lynch

One of the finest lessons nature can teach us is that of hope. She shows us hope realized with every bud that blossoms and every bird that learns to fly. ~ Author unknown

Optimism is the faith that leads to achievement. Nothing can be done without hope and confidence. ~ Helen Keller

Patience with others is Love, Patience with self is Hope, Patience with God is Faith. ~ Adel Bestavros

Practice hope. As hopefulness becomes a habit, you can achieve a permanently happy spirit. ~ Norman Vincent Peale

Strong hope is a much greater stimulant to life than any single realized joy could be. ~ Friedrich Nietzsche

The capacity for hope is the most significant fact of life. It provides human beings with a sense of destination and the energy to get started. ~ Norman Cousins

The first task of a leader is to keep hope alive. ~ Joe Batten

The future belongs to those who give the next generation reason for hope. ~ Pierre Teilhard de Chardin

The human body experiences a powerful gravitational pull in the direction of hope. That is why the patient's hopes are the physician's secret weapon. They are the hidden ingredients in any prescription. ~ Norman Cousins

The natural flights of the human mind are not from pleasure to pleasure but from hope to hope. ~ Samuel Johnson

There are three things I was born with in this world, and there are three things I will have until the day I die – hope, determination, and song. ~ Miriam Makeba

There is no medicine like hope, no incentive so great, and no tonic so powerful as expectation of something tomorrow. ~ Orison Swett Marden

Three grand essentials to happiness in this life are something to do, something to love, and something to hope for. ~ Joseph Addison

True hope dwells on the possible, even when life seems to be a plot written by someone who wants to see how much adversity we can overcome. ~ Walter Anderson

We judge of man's wisdom by his hope. ~ Ralph Waldo Emerson

We live by admiration, hope, and love. ~ William Wordsworth

We must accept finite disappointment, but we must never lose infinite hope. ~ Dr. Martin Luther King Jr.

We want to create hope for the person ... we must give hope, always hope. ~ Mother Teresa

When the world says, "Give up," Hope whispers, "Try it one more time." ~ Author Unknown

Whether we be young or old, Our destiny, our being's heart, and home,
Is with infinitude, and only there; With hope, it is, hope that can never die,
Effort and expectation, and desire,
And something evermore about to be. ~ William Wordsworth

While there's life, there's hope. ~ Cicero

You are here in order to enable the world to live more amply, with greater vision, with a finer spirit of hope and achievement. ~ Woodrow Wilson

ACKNOWLEDGMENTS

Thank you Shareen Baker at Creativeimpact for the book cover design. You make all things beautiful.

Thank you to Cyana Gaffney for your help in prepping this book for publishing and your encouragement that the content would be helpful.

Thank you to Glori, Sarah, Sheila, Joanne, Vahen, Wendy, Katelyn, and Brenda, for your friendship and vulnerability in sharing your stories. Kristen Fersovitch and Phyllis Fisher will hear our thanks in heaven.

Thank you to Jocelyn Jones for not killing me during the journey to write, edit, research, edit, proof, edit, and publish.

BOB'S BOOKS

ORNAMENT: THE FAITH, HOPE, AND JOY OF KRISTEN FERSOVITCH (2015)

ORNAMENT is an answer to the question many people asked after they heard Kristen Fersovitch's story or her songs - "How could I have a faith like Kristen's?" Like a beautiful Christmas tree ornament, Kristen's life was on display for all to see. She was diagnosed with inoperable cancer at age 28 with a husband and three boys under the age of five. A singer and songwriter, Kristen commanded any stage she performed on and won the hearts of all who encountered her extraordinary life.

"ORNAMENT beautifully challenges the assumption that life has to be perfect to find joy; that circumstance have to work out in our favour to maintain our faith. It breaks the bonds of despair by showing who is able to bring real HOPE! If you need help finding that kind of hope; a redemption not yet visible-you need this book!"

"Truly amazing story of a loving, exceptional mother and her family. A touching book that teaches how to find strength in our darkest moments and reminds us just how precious life is."

PHYLLIS: LOVE NEVER LETS GO (2018)

"Some people come into our lives and quickly go. Some stay for a while and leave footprints on our hearts, and we are never the same again." Phyllis was that kind of friend. People who knew her will never be the same again.

A memoir of Rev. Phyllis Fisher written as a legacy piece for her grandchildren now read throughout the world. Phyllis was one of the longest living kidney transplant patients and had a second transplant later in life. She courageously battled cancer. A loving wife and devoted mom to two adopted children and grandmother to four grandchildren. Phyllis served in church ministry for over four decades as a pastor's wife and chaplain.

Purchase your copy by emailing bob@revwords.com or online at Chapters.ca or Amazon.ca

AUTHOR PAGE

Bob Jones is a recovering perfectionist who collects Coca-Cola memorabilia and drinks Iced Tea. His office walls are adorned with his sons' framed football jerseys and his bookshelves with soul food.

Bob is a communicator, excelling in preaching and now making his mark as an author. His first book, *Ornament: The Faith, Hope, and Joy of Kristen Fersovitch* won the Word Alive award for Life Story in 2016. In 2018 he wrote the memoir, *Phyllis: Love Never Lets Go* as a tribute to Rev. Bruce and Phyllis Fisher. His articles appear regularly in the Testimony magazine, and the St Albert Gazette, he blogs monthly for Word Alive Publishing and Inscribe Writers.

In 2019 he and Jocelyn started REVwords.com because words matter. They share hope for people facing cancer, mental illness, and loss. Together they operate *Supporting the Fighters* a group to help women fighting cancer.

Bob has been married to Jocelyn for 40 years, a father of two plus two and a grampa of five. He has served as a pastor with the Pentecostal Assemblies of Canada in Ontario, Quebec, and Alberta over four decades. His passion is shepherding people through the highs and heartaches of life. He is a marathoner and is devoted to running his race of life as a champion.

Manufactured by Amazon.ca
Bolton, ON

34300701R00088